◆—SEAFOOD—◆

◆

A Collection of Heart-Healthy Recipes

By Janis Harsila, R.D. & Evie Hansen

Design by Lisa R. Sowder
Illustrations by Stephen Spencer
Cover photo courtesy of Alaska Seafood Marketing Institute
Typesetting by Typehouse
Printing by BookCrafters — Chelsea, Michigan

Special thanks to:
American Heart Association — Washington Affiliate
National Marine Fisheries Service
Seafood Business Report

National Seafood Educators
P.O. Box 60006
Richmond Beach, WA 98160
(206) 546-6410

Printed in the United States of America

First Edition
Fourth Printing October 1987

TABLE OF CONTENTS

ALL ABOUT SEAFOOD

Coronary heart disease is the United State's number one killer. Mounting scientific evidence continues to suggest that most people can reduce their risk of developing coronary heart disease by eating a heart healthy diet. In fact, research shows that for every 1 percent decrease in blood cholesterol levels, heart attack risk decreases by 2 percent!

"SEAFOOD: A Collection of Heart-Healthy Recipes" is designed to introduce people to heart healthy seafood cooking in a practical, step-by-step way with recipes that are light, but delicious. Helpful hints and ideas include steps from buying to preparation to make seafood cooking less mysterious to the novice.

All recipes have been tested in our kitchens.

All recipes follow the American Heart Association's dietary guidelines. Recipes are:
Low in calories
Low in total fat, saturated fat and cholesterol
Low to moderately low in sodium
Include a 3½-4 ounce portion of seafood

SEAFOOD: THE HEART- HEALTHY PROTEIN CHOICE

Seafood consumption is on the upswing. Choosing SEAFOOD as a heart healthy protein choice is becoming a trend in this country, and for very good reasons. Most seafood is:

- Low in calories: a 3½ ounce serving of white-fleshed fish contains less than 100 calories.
- High in protein: a 3½ ounce serving of seafood supplies about half the total protein required by the body each day.
- Low in total fat, saturated fat and cholesterol.
- Fish oils are high in polyunsaturated fats and omega-3 fatty acids that decrease cholesterol.
- Low in sodium.
- A good source of vitamins and minerals such as thiamin, riboflavin, pantothenic acid, niacin, phosphorus, potassium, iron, iodine, fluoride, zinc, selenium and copper.
- Easily digested: seafood lends itself well to the diets of children and the elderly.
- Quick and easy to prepare.

The American Heart Association recommends the following guidelines to reduce your risk of heart disease and lower cholesterol and triglyceride levels:

1. Meet your daily need for protein, vitamins and other nutrients. It is always important to eat a well-balanced diet to include all food groups.
2. Achieve and maintain ideal body weight by controlling calorie intake.
3. Avoid eating excessive amounts of food containing saturated fat and cholesterol.
4. Eat less total fat and when fat is used to choose polyunsaturated fats and oils.
5. Limit salt intake to less than 1 teaspoon per day.
6. Avoid cigarette smoking.
7. Exercise regularly.

NUTRITIONAL BREAKDOWN OF SEAFOOD

100 grams (3½ oz.) raw, edible portion	Calories	Protein grams	Fat grams	Sodium mgs	Cholesterol mgs	Omega-3 fatty acids gms
Albacore tuna	102	18.2	3.0	50	25	1.3
Catfish	103	17.6	3.1	60	55	.3
Clams	80	11.0	1.5	80	40	trace
Cod	70	16.7	.7	70	40	.2
Crab, dungeness	81	17.3	1.3	266	90	.3
Crab, imitation	90	13.4	.1	600	50	—
Crab, king	75	15.2	.8	70	60	—
Croaker	85	18.0	.8	80	50	.2
Dogfish, spiny (Pacific shark)	155	17.6	9.0	100	40	1.9
Flounder	90	18.1	1.4	56	50	.2
Grouper	87	19.3	.5	80	—	.3
Haddock	80	18.2	.5	60	60	—
Halibut	105	20.9	1.2	60	50	.4
Herring	150	18.3	8.5	75	80	1.7
Langostinos	74	8.2	1.6	—	—	—
Lobster	90	16.9	1.9	210	85	.2
Mackerel	160	21.9	7.3	80	40	2.5
Mahi Mahi	102	21.0	1.0	130	85	—
Monkfish	70	15.5	1.0	—	35	—
Mussels	75	12.2	1.6	80	25	.5
Ocean perch	95	19.0	1.5	70	60	.2
Octopus	76	15.0	1.5	—	122	.2
Orange roughy	65	14.7	.3	—	—	—
Oysters	70	14.2	1.2	75	50	.6
Pollock	85	19.5	.8	60	50	.5
Rockfish (snapper)	97	18.9	1.8	50	40	.5
Sablefish (black cod, butter fish)	130	17.9	5.7	55	65	1.5
Salmon	142	20.0	7.0	50	65	1.1
Scallops	82	15.3	.2	160	50	.2
Shark, thrasher	90	20.0	1.0	50	—	—
Shrimp	90	18.8	.8	140	158	.3
Skate	95	20.0	1.0	—	—	—
Sole	70	14.9	.5	55	45	—
Squid	85	16.4	.9	160	—	.3
Swordfish	120	19.4	4.4	70	50	.2
Tilefish	90	18.6	1.2	—	—	—
Trout, rainbow	195	21.5	11.4	52	50	.5
Whiting	95	21.3	1.2	50	20	.4

NOTE: Use these figures only as a guide. Values vary with species, water temperature, catch location, season caught, etc.

— Unreliable statistics

OMEGA-3 FATTY ACIDS

Exciting research in the last 20 years shows that along with seafood containing high amounts of polyunsaturated oils, these oils contain significant amounts of omega-3 fatty acids. Omega-3 fatty acids are long-chained poly-unsaturated fats which occur mainly in the oils of seafood and marine animals. These fats tend to lower blood cholesterol and triglyceride levels. Omega-3 fatty acids also interfere in a desirable way with platelet functions that contribute to formation of clots in arteries. Thus, the blood's thinner and les likely to clot.

Reports from Denmark in the early 1970's first associated the low incidence of cardiovascular disease among Greenland Eskimos with their high intake of fish and fish oils. Many research projects have been triggered as a result of these findings.

Omega-3 fatty acids are being studied to determine their affects on the human body — as well as, the benefits and risks of including increased amounts in the diet. Ongoing research include omega-3 fatty acids:

- Apparent protective role against heart disease and role in lowering blood cholesterol and triglyceride levels.
- Mechanisms that lead to blood thinning.
- Possible benefits in inflammatory diseases, such as rheumatoid arthritis, as well as, possible relief in other auto-immune diseases such as lupus erythematosus.
- Possible benefits in protection from some cancers.
- Amounts of omega-3 fatty acids that can be safely consumed in the diet for maximum benefits without disadvantages.

Eating a well-balanced heart healthy diet and making appropriate changes in lifestyles are key steps in decreasing your risk of developing heart disease.

A great deal of research is needed to fully understand how omega-3 fatty acids do what they do. But a full understanding of omega-3 fatty acid benefits is not necessary to see the important changes in eating habits suggested by research already done.

According to the *New England Journal of Medicine* (May, 1985),

"it seems justifiable to include a recommendation for one to two fish dishes a week in dietary guidelines for the prevention of coronary heart disease."

NOTE: Fish oil supplements or capsules cannot be recommended at this time, except in very special controlled circumstances. Health risks of fish oils may include:
  — Adverse affects on blood clotting
  — Possible toxic levels of vitamins A & D
  — Possible presence of environmental contaminants and other undesirable compounds
  — Possible increased vitamin E requirements

†††At this time, it is safer, less expensive and more enjoyable to obtain omega-3 fatty acids from a meal of seafood!

CREATIVE IDEAS TO INTRODUCE SEAFOOD TO HESITANT FRIENDS AND FAMILY!

1. Modify a favorite family recipe.

2. Serve your family a meal of their favorite dishes with a portion of seafood.

3. For those who are wary of fish bones: buy boneless fish fillets or have seafood service person debone fish for you. Any fish can be made boneless by pulling out the bones with a needle nose plier, just like they do in restaurants. Common boneless fish: orange roughy, Alaskan jumbo cod, monkfish

4. Try new and exciting recipes that include seafood, such as "Italian Cioppino" with wonderful flavors that kids love.

5. For the steak and potato lover, start with a firm-fleshed fish, such as swordfish, halibut, fresh tuna or shark.

TEN "MUST TRY" RECIPES

Listed are 10 recipes that are especially good. These recipes are easy to prepare and are a good starting point for the cook who is unfamiliar with seafood cookery, or who wants an alternative to "fried fish."

Italian Cioppino, page 60
Steamed Mussels or Clams, page 26
Hot Seafood Salad, page 42
Easy Shrimp and Pea Salad, page 49
Sesame Prawns, page 120
Orange Roughy with Oriental Sauce, page 82
Poached Cod with Herbs, page 68
Halibut in Tarragon, page 75
Sauteed Orange Roughy, page 83
Broiled Salmon Steaks with Herb Sauce, page 95

COOKING RULE:
TEN MINUTES PER INCH

One easy rule for cooking fish is to cook fish 10 minutes per 1 inch of thickness. (To determine thickness, measure thickest part of fish with a ruler.) Double cooking time for frozen fish. The ten minutes rule applies for all cooking methods except microwaving.

Remember, fish cooks quickly. Fish is cooked when the flesh becomes opaque and just begins to flake when tested with a fork. Overcooking tends to toughen and dry out the flesh.

EDIBILITY PROFILE

This profile, developed by the National Marine Fisheries Service, groups finfish with similar color and flavor characteristics. If a certain species is unavailable, another in the same category may work well in the same recipe.

White Meat Very light, delicate flavor	*White Meat* Light to moderate flavor	*Light Meat* Very light, delicate flavor
Pacific sanddab	Pacific whiting	Shovelnose
Cod	Spotted sea trout	Sturgeon
Cusk	Butterfish	Smelt
Haddock	Whiting	Alaska pollock
Spotted cabrilla	Sauger	Pacific Ocean
Lake whitefish	Red snapper	perch
Southern flounder	American plaice	Brook trout
Dover sole	Wolffish	Walleye
Petrale sole	Gray triggerfish	Rainbow trout
Rex sole	Catfish	Giant sea bass
Summer flounder	Lingcod	Grouper
Yellowtail flounder	White sea trout	White sea bass
Witch flounder	Cobia	Bluegill
Yellowtail snapper	English sole	White crappie
Pacific halibut	Winter flounder	Tautog
Tilefish	Snook	
	Arrowtooth flounder	
	Mahi mahi	

Light Meat Light to moderate flavor		*Light Meat* More pronounced flavor	*Darker Meat* Light to moderate flavor
Atlantic salmon	Buffalofish	Atlantic mackerel	Black sea bass
Pink salmon	Jewfish	King mackerel	Ocean pout
Lake sturgeon	Lake herring	Spanish mackerel	Chinook salmon
Monkfish	Croaker	Redeye mullet	(Red) Sockeye
Sculpin	Chum salmon	Blue runner	salmon
Atlantic Ocean	Pompano		Bluefish
perch	Striped bass		
Scup	Sand shark		
Northern pike	Vermillion		
Burbot	snapper		
Rockfish	Perch		
Pollock	Lake trout		
Carp	Mullet		
Swordfish	Coho salmon		
Black drum	Crevalle jack		
Greenland turbo	Eel		
Spot	Sablefish		
Sheepshead	Lake chub		

BASIC PREPARATION TECHNIQUES FOR HEART-HEALTHY SEAFOOD
"Fast and Easy to Fix!"

POACHING: Poaching is as easy as boiling water. Estimate amount of liquid needed to barely cover a single layer of fish in a saucepan or frying pan. Suggested liquids include skim milk, water or wine. Season liquid with chopped carrots, celery, onions and peppercorns. Bring seasoned liquid to a boil. Cover and simmer about 10 minutes. Add fish. Simmer until done. Poaching is an easy method of preparing fish for the beginning cook.

STEAMING: Place seafood on a steaming rack set 2 inches above boiling liquid in a deep pot. Season as desired. Cover tightly. Reduce heat and steam until done. Mollusks, such as mussels and clams and other seafoods are excellent when steamed.

BAKING: Place seafood in a baking dish. Add sauce or topping to keep moist. Cover and bake at 400° until done.

BROILING: Place seafood on a broiler pan. Brush with a small amount of melted polyunsaturated margarine and lemon juice. Flavor with herbs and spices, such as pepper and dill weed. Broil 4-5 inches from heat source without turning. Cook until done.

SAUTEING: Heat a small amount of polyunsaturated margarine or oil with liquid, such as white wine, in a frying pan. Add chopped mushrooms, green onions, lemon juice and seafood to liquid. Sauté over medium high heat until done.

MICROWAVING: Place seafood in a non-metal dish and cover with plastic wrap. Cook approximately three minutes per pound or follow manufacturer's directions. A helpful hint to successful microwaving is to turn under any thin portions of the fillets, so that the thickness is the same for all pieces. Another suggestion is to microwave in microwavable plastic bag.

HOW TO CUT FISH

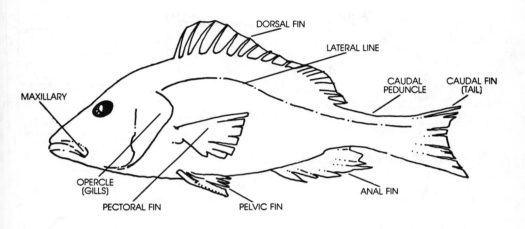

DORSAL FIN

LATERAL LINE

CAUDAL PEDUNCLE

CAUDAL FIN (TAIL)

MAXILLARY

OPERCLE (GILLS)

PECTORAL FIN

PELVIC FIN

ANAL FIN

DRAWN

Drawn fish are whole fish that have been scaled and have had entrails removed. Head and fins are intact. A drawn fish has longer storage life than a round fish (sold just as it comes from the water), because entrails cause rapid spoilage.

DRESSED/PAN-DRESSED

Dressed fish have been scaled, gutted, and had gills removed. Head and fins are intact. A dressed fish is often cooked in one piece, by baking, poaching, or barbecuing. A pan-dressed fish has head, tail, fins, and viscera removed.

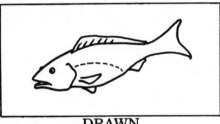

FILLETED

Fillets are the boneless or pinbone-in sides of a fish, cut away from the backbone and removed in one piece.

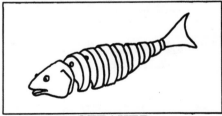

STEAKED

Steaks are cross-section cuts from dressed fish. They are generally 1–1½ inches thick. Large fish such as salmon, halibut, and swordfish are often steaked.

15

HOW TO FILLET A ROUND-BODIED FISH

1. With fish facing away from you, use a sharp, thin-bladed knife to cut along the back of the fish, from tail to head. Make a second cut just behind the gills, down to the backbone.

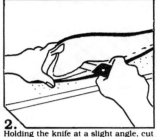

2. Holding the knife at a slight angle, cut along the bone to free the back side of the fillet.

3. Peel back the free meat, then cut fillet away from rib cage. Turn fish over and repeat above steps for second fillet.

HOW TO STEAK A SALMON

1. Remove fins from cleaned, scaled fish by running knife point along each side of fin base, then pulling fins free. To remove head, make diagonal cut behind the gills and sever backbone with heavy knife or cleaver.

2. Still using a heavy knife, slice fish into steaks about 1 inch thick, starting about 4 inches from the head end. (Reserve unsteaked head-and-tail portions for another use.)

HOW TO FILLET A FLAT FISH

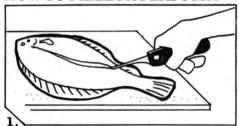

1. With the eyed (dark) side of the flatfish up, use a flexible boning knife to make a cut along the spine from the gills to the tail.

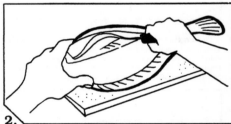

2. Slide the blade between backbone and flesh, lifting the fillet away from the bone. Remove the second fillet in the same manner.

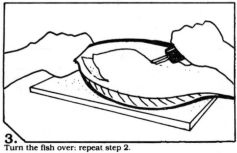

3. Turn the fish over; repeat step 2.

4. To skin, grasp fillet by the tail end, skin side down. Holding the knife at a slight angle, cut the meat free.

16

HOW TO OPEN A CLAM

1.
Wash clams thoroughly, discarding any that have broken shells or that do not close. Wearing a heavy glove for safety, hold the clam in your palm and force the blade of a clam knife between the shells.

2.
Run the knife around the edge of the shell to cut through the muscles holding it together.

3.
Open clam and remove top shell. Use knife to loosen clam from bottom shell. Check for shell fragments before serving.

HOW TO SHUCK AN OYSTER

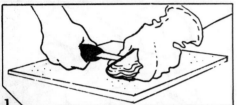

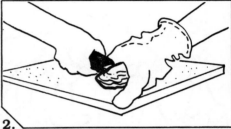

1.
Hold oysters under cold running water and scrub with a stiff brush; discard those that are not tightly closed or that do not close quickly when handled. Place oyster, cupped side down, on a firm surface, holding it (with a gloved hand) near the hinge.

2.
Insert an oyster knife in the side opposite the hinge, and twist knife blade to force oyster open.

3.
Run the knife around the edge of the shell to cut the muscle that holds the two shells together.

4.
Remove top shell, and loosen oyster from bottom shell. Check for shell fragments before serving.

HOW TO CLEAN A MUSSEL

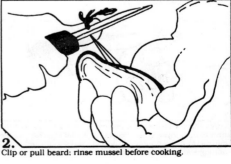

1.
Prepare mussels as soon as possible after gathering. If mussels must be stored, refrigerate them at 35°F. to 40°F. To prepare, scrub shells in cold water to remove grass and mud. Discard those that have open shells or shells that do not close quickly with handling.

2.
Clip or pull beard; rinse mussel before cooking.

HOW TO DRESS A SOFT-SHELL CRAB

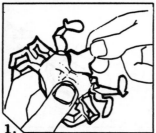

1. Remove the apron, the segmented abdominal part beneath the carapace, or shell.

2. Lift the carapace's pointed ends, and remove spongy material.

3. Using scissors, cut about ½ inch behind the eyes and remove the face of the crab. What remains is the edible portion.

HOW TO CRACK A CRAB

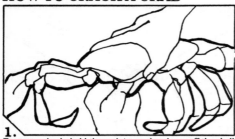

1. To remove back, hold the crab in one hand, pry off the shell with the other.

2. Using a small, heavy knife, cut away the gills. Wash out the intestines and spongy matter.

3. Break off the claws and crack them with the knife handle, a mallet, or the back of a cleaver. Use the knife to pry meat out if necessary. Twist legs loose from the body, crack them, and remove meat.

4. Cut the body down the middle, then cut halves into several parts. Use the point of the knife to remove the lump of meat from each side of the rear portion of the body.

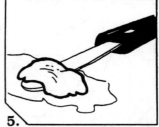

5. Remove the remainder of the meat by prying upward with the knife.

HOW TO CLEAN A SHRIMP

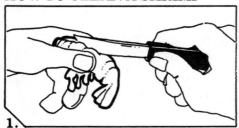

1. With a sharp knife, make a shallow cut along the back of the shrimp, from head to tail. Peel off shell and legs, leaving the shell on the tail, if desired. To devein, hold shrimp under cold running water. The water will help rinse out the vein.

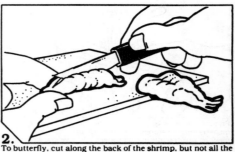

2. To butterfly, cut along the back of the shrimp, but not all the way through. Spread the halves open.

HOW TO DRESS A LOBSTER

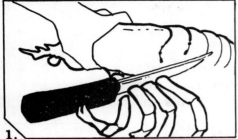 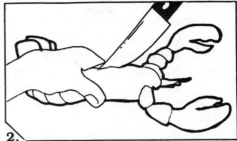

1. For lobster that is to be broiled, rather than boiled live. Cut off legs.

2. Insert a knife in the abdomen, and cut through the under-shell toward the head, leaving back shell intact.

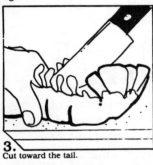 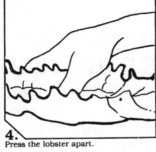 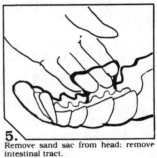

3. Cut toward the tail.

4. Press the lobster apart.

5. Remove sand sac from head; remove intestinal tract.

HOW TO DRESS A SQUID

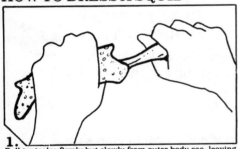 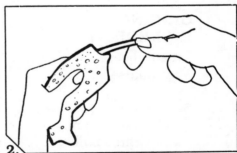

1. Pull tentacles firmly but slowly from outer body sac, leaving body intact. Intestines should come out with tentacles.

2. From body sac, pull out and discard thin, transparent quill.

 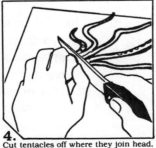 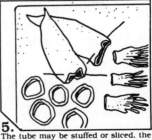

3. Peel away speckled outer membrane covering sac and fins. Turn body sac inside out, and rinse.

4. Cut tentacles off where they join head, and discard head.

5. The tube may be stuffed or sliced, the tentacles chopped and included in stuffing or in a marinated salad.

19

A WELL-BALANCED DIET

A well-balanced diet includes:
   Fruits and vegetables
   Legumes (beans and peas)
   Seafood, veal and poultry and less red meat
   Whole grains and enriched bread and cereal products
   Lean dairy products, such as skim milk and low fat
      cheeses
   Fats and oils in limited amounts

Variety and moderation are important to the total diet.

RECIPE SUBSTITUTIONS FOR A HEART-HEALTHY DIET

Preparing a heart healthy meal can be easy. The following list provides basic substitutions that can be used to make your own recipes heart healthy. Many of these substitutions were used in "SEAFOOD: A Collection of Heart-Healthy Recipes" to lower calorie, fat and sodium levels.

ORIGINAL INGREDIENT	HEART HEALTY SUBSTITUTION
Cream cheese	blended cottage cheese
Mayonnaise	low fat cottage cheese or low fat yogurt
Sour cream	low fat yogurt
Whole milk, cream, evaporated milk	skim milk, evaporated skim milk
Whole milk cottage cheese	low fat cottage cheese
Butter, lard	polyunsaturated oils and margarines made with: corn cottonseed safflower sesame seed soybean sunflower

Cheddar cheese	part-skim mozzarella cheese, Farmer's cheese, part-skim ricotta cheese
salt, onion salt, garlic salt	Herbs and spices can be combined in creative ways to make seafood recipes more flavorful. Instead of using your salt shaker, try cooking seafood with these herbs and spices to enhance its flavor:

allspice	garlic powder
basil	marjoram
bay leaf	mustard
cayenne	nutmeg
pepper	onion powder
celery seed	oregano
celery leaves	paprika
chervil	parsley
curry powder	rosemary
dill seed	saffron
or weed	tarragon
fennel seed	thyme

¼ teaspoon powdered herbs = ¼-1 teaspoon crumbled herbs = 2 teaspoons fresh herbs

Other seasonings to complement seafood: lemon, wine, light soy sauce

GREAT BEGINNINGS

BAKED MUSHROOMS WITH IMITATION CRAB

2 tablespoons polyunsaturated margarine
4 tablespoons green onion, finely chopped
1 clove garlic, finely minced
1½ cups imitation crab flakes
2 tablespoons ricotta cheese
1 teaspoon lemon juice
2 tablespoons bread crumbs
white pepper
¼ cup water
18-24 large mushroom tops

Melt margarine in 8-10 inch skillet over moderate heat. Sauté green onion and garlic, stirring constantly, for 2 minutes. Stir in crab, ricotta cheese, lemon juice, bread crumbs and white pepper and toss with onions for 10 seconds. Lightly oil a 9x13 inch pan and add ¼ cup water. Place mushroom tops in one layer and spoon on crab filling. Cover and bake in 350° oven for 15-20 minutes until mushrooms are tender when pierced with knife and filling is bubbly. Serve on platter. Makes 6 servings.

110 calories per serving
5 grams fat per serving
385 mg sodium per serving
25 mg cholesterol per serving

STEAMED
MUSSELS OR CLAMS

36 mussels or steamer clams in shells
2 tablespoons polyunsaturated margarine
1 cup white wine
½ cup green onion, chopped
¼ cup parsley, chopped
2 cloves garlic, minced

Scrub clams or debeard mussels. (To debeard mussels, clip beard off with scissors just before cooking.) Melt margarine with wine in 8-quart saucepan. Add green onion, parsley and garlic to wine sauce. Place clams or mussels in saucepan. Cover with tight lid. Steam on medium heat for approximately 10 minutes or until shells open. Agitate the pan during this time to cook the clams or mussels evenly. The broth is delicious to drink. Serves 6 as appetizers.

A delicious entree idea that will serve 2-3 people.

120 calories per serving
5 grams fat per serving
165 mg sodium per serving
20 mg cholesterol per serving

OYSTERS ON THE HALF SHELL WITH RED WINE VINEGAR SAUCE

24 oysters in the shell

Sauce:
5 oz. red wine vinegar
2 tablespoons olive oil
3 tablespoons shallots or green onion, finely minced

Clean oysters by scrubbing under cold running water. Open with an oyster knife. Free the oyster and leave on the half shell. To make sauce: Mix vinegar, oil and onions for dressing. Serve oysters with sauce on the side. Makes 8 servings.

65 calories per serving
4 grams fat per serving
30 mg sodium per serving
25 mg cholesterol per serving

← SALMON-STUFFED → PASTA SHELLS

1 - 8 oz. package conch-shaped pasta shells
¼ teaspoon salt
2 beaten eggs
2 cups ricotta cheese
½ cup green pepper, finely chopped
¼ cup onion, finely chopped
¼ cup fresh parsley, finely chopped
¼ cup skim milk
½ teaspoon lemon peel, finely grated
1 - 15½ oz. can salmon, drained and flaked
⅓ cup fine dry bread crumbs
⅓ cup Parmesan cheese, grated
2 tablespoons polyunsaturated margarine, melted

Cook pasta, uncovered, in a large amount of boiling salted water until tender; drain and set aside. In a medium bowl combine eggs, ricotta cheese, green pepper, onion, chopped parsley, milk and lemon peel. Stir in salmon. Spoon mixture into cooked shells. Place shells, filled side up, in a 9x13 inch baking dish. Add 2 tablespoons water to dish. Cover and bake at 350° for 30 minutes. Combine the bread crumbs, Parmesan cheese and melted margarine; sprinkle over shells. Bake, uncovered, 5 minutes more. Serve hot. Garnish with lemon and lime wedges and parsley, if desired. Makes 30 appetizers.

100 calories per appetizer
3.3 grams fat per appetizer
90 mg sodium per appetizer
30 mg cholesterol per appetizer

SEVICHE

1½ lbs. scallops, or other white-fleshed fish fillets
1 cup fresh lime juice
2 tomatoes, peeled, seeded and diced
½ cup red onion, grated
pepper to taste
¼ teaspoon salt
¼ cup olive oil
parsley or cilantro

Dice raw fish and cover with lime juice for at least 2 hours or overnight. Drain. Mix fish with remaining ingredients. Serve very cold in prechilled cocktail glasses. Garnish with parsley. Makes 8 servings.

150 calories per serving
7 grams fat per serving
285 mg sodium per serving
40 mg cholesterol per serving

HOLIDAY FISH SPREAD

1 - 15½ oz. can salmon or 2 cups cooked white-fleshed fish
8 oz. low fat cottage cheese
2 tablespoons onion, finely chopped
1 tablespoon parsley, minced
½ cup almonds, finely chopped
1 teaspoon liquid smoke
¼ teaspoon pepper
1 tablespoon lemon juice
1 teaspoon prepared horseradish
¼ teaspoon garlic powder
2 tablespoons red or green pepper, finely chopped

Blend cottage cheese until smooth using a food processor or blender. Add remaining ingredients and combine. Chill several hours or overnight. Excellent as a spread on dark rye bread with cucumber slice. Serve in stuffed celery sticks or as a dip for raw vegetables. Makes about 3 cups or 48 appetizer sandwiches.

with white-fleshed fish:
18 calories per tablespoon
1 gram fat per tablespoon
18 mg sodium per tablespoon
10 mg cholesterol per tablespoon

with salmon:
29 calories per tablespoon
1.6 grams fat per tablespoon
65 mg sodium per tablespoon
10 mg cholesterol per tablespoon

SKEWERED SCALLOPS

1 lb. scallops
2 large green peppers
1 pint cherry tomatoes

Sauce:
1/3 cup lemon juice
3 tablespoons honey
3 tablespoons prepared mustard
2 tablespoons polyunsaturated oil
1 1/2 teaspoons curry powder

Cut large scallops in half. Cut green peppers into 1-inch squares. Alternate scallops, tomatoes and green pepper on 40 skewers or round toothpicks, approximately 3 inches long. Place kabobs on lightly-oiled broiler pan. To make sauce: Combine sauce ingredients. Brush kabobs with sauce. Broil about 4 inches from source of heat for 5 minutes. Turn carefully and brush with sauce. Broil about 5 minutes longer, basting once. Makes approximately 40 kabobs.

20 calories per kabob
1 gram fat per kabob
35 mg sodium per kabob
4 mg cholesterol per kabob

◆— SALMON MOUSSE —◆

2 egg whites
1/4 teaspoon cream of tartar
2 envelopes unflavored gelatin
3/4 cup cold water
1 - 15 1/2 oz. can salmon
1 cup low fat cottage cheese, small curd
1/2 cup plain low fat yogurt
3/4 cup green onion, minced
1/2 cup celery, chopped
1 tablespoon lemon juice
1/2 teaspoon horseradish
1/4 teaspoon ground red pepper (cayenne)
dash hot red pepper sauce
nonstick cooking spray
radishes, cucumber slices and lemon wedges for garnish

Place egg whites and cream of tartar in a small bowl. Let warm to room temperature. In a small saucepan sprinkle gelatin over cold water; let stand 5 minutes to soften. Stir over low heat until gelatin is completely dissolved. Remove from heat; turn into medium bowl; cool to room temperature. Drain salmon. In food processor or with electric blender process salmon, cottage cheese, yogurt and horseradish until smooth and pastelike — about 1 minute. Turn into bowl with gelatin. Stir green onion, celery, lemon juice, red pepper (cayenne), and red pepper sauce into salmon mixture. Beat egg whites to stiff peaks and fold into salmon mixture. Spray a 1-quart fish mold with nonstick cooking spray. Turn salmon mixture into mold. Refrigerate 3-4 hours or until firm. Unmold mixture. To garnish: cut several radishes into thin slices; place 2 slices for eyes; cut remaining slices in quarters; overlap on surface of salmon mousse to simulate scales. Garnish serving plate with additional radishes, cucumber slices and lemon wedges. Makes 10 servings.

80 calories per serving
2.3 grams fat per serving
210 mg sodium per serving
65 mg cholesterol per serving

JUDY'S TUNA OR SALMON PUFFS

2 - 7 oz. cans tuna or salmon
2 cups celery, finely chopped
¼ cup mayonnaise
¼ cup low fat yogurt
2 tablespoons onion, finely chopped
2 tablespoons sweet pickle, chopped
Puff shells

Drain and flake fish. Combine all ingredients except puff shells. Mix thoroughly. Cut tops from puff shells. Fill each puff shell with approximately 2 teaspoonfuls of salad. Makes approximately 72 puffs.

Puff Shells
1 cup boiling water
½ cup polyunsaturated margarine
1 cup flour
4 eggs

Combine water and margarine in a saucepan and bring to a boil. Add flour all at one time and stir vigorously, until mixture forms a ball and leaves the sides of the pan. Remove from heat. Add eggs, one at a time, beating thoroughly after each addition. Continue beating until a stiff dough is formed. Drop by level teaspoonfuls on a cooking sheet. Bake in a very hot oven, 450° for 10 minutes. Reduce heat to 350° and continue baking about 10 minutes longer. Let cool completely, before filling. Makes approximately 72 puff shells.

38 calories per filled puff
2.3 grams fat per filled puff
50 mg sodium per filled puff
20 mg cholesterol per filled puff

◆— SHRIMP STUFFED —➤ CELERY

1 - 7 oz. can shrimp
⅓ cup low calorie mayonnaise (or regular mayonnaise)
1½ tablespoons lemon juice
2 tablespoons parsley flakes
1½ tablespoons onion, finely chopped
⅓ cup crushed pineapple
2 tablespoons walnuts, chopped
¼ teaspoon salt (optional)
4 drops Tabasco sauce
6 celery stalks
dash paprika

In a 1-quart bowl, combine all ingredients except celery and paprika. Mix until well blended. Fill celery sticks with mixture. Sprinkle with paprika. Cut into 2-inch lengths. Makes 8-10 servings as an appetizer.

70 calories per serving
2 grams fat per serving
145 mg sodium per serving
50 mg cholesterol per serving

SALMON/TUNA COTTAGE CHEESE SPREAD

1 - 7 oz. can tuna or salmon
2 cups low fat cottage cheese
¼ cup green onion, finely chopped
¼ cup green pepper, finely chopped
2 tablespoons pimiento, finely chopped
1 tablespoon Worcestershire sauce
celery, green pepper or cucumber

Drain and flake fish; place in a medium bowl. Add cottage cheese, onions, green pepper, pimiento and Worcestershire sauce; mix well. Cover and chill 1-2 hours. Serve as an appetizer and spread on celery chunks, green pepper wedges or cucumber slices, etc., or use as a salad to stuff green pepper halves or tomatoes. Can also be used as a topping for baked potatoes. Makes 6 salad servings or 48 appetizers.

130 calories per serving
4.5 grams fat per serving
385 mg sodium per serving
20 mg cholesterol per serving

SMOKEY SALMON PATÉ

1 - 15½ oz. can salmon
⅔ cup low fat cottage cheese
¼ teaspoon liquid smoke flavoring
1 tablespoon lemon juice
2 tablespoons onion, minced
2 tablespoons ripe olives, finely chopped
1 teaspoon Worcestershire sauce
½ teaspoon paprika

Drain salmon and chop very fine or mash with a fork. Press cottage cheese through a sieve or blend smooth and combine with salmon and remaining ingredients. Mix well. Cover and chill for at least one hour. Serve with melba toast or rye bread. Makes 2½ cups or 40 appetizers.

20 calories per serving
1 gram fat per serving
75 mg sodium per serving
6 grams cholesterol per serving

SALADS

SPRING SALAD

1 - 7¾ oz. can salmon
½ lb. fresh asparagus or broccoli

Marinade:
2 tablespoons polyunsaturated oil
1½ tablespoons lemon juice
dash white pepper

Dressing:
½ cup low fat yogurt
¼ cup low fat cottage cheese
¼ teaspoon tarragon
parsley, chopped

1 tablespoon green onion, chopped
salad greens
tomato wedges
radish roses
celery, sliced

Chill can of salmon. Steam asparagus or broccoli just until tender-crisp. To prepare marinade: Combine oil, lemon juice and pepper. Pour over asparagus or broccoli. Marinate in refrigerator 1 hour. Drain, reserving marinade. To prepare dressing: Combine marinade with yogurt, cottage cheese and tarragon. Blend. Place in dish and sprinkle with parsley. Drain salmon and break into chunks with a fork. Arrange salmon and asparagus or broccoli on platter lined with green onion and crisp greens. Garnish with tomato wedges, radish roses and celery and pour dressing over salad. Makes 4 servings.

200 calories per serving
11.6 grams fat per serving
275 mg sodium per serving
30 mg cholesterol per serving

◆── SOUSED SALMON ──◆

2-7¾ oz. cans salmon
2 tablespoons capers
½ small red onion, thinly sliced in rings
¼ cup white wine vinegar

◆

8 whole bibb lettuce
olives
cucumber slices
asparagus spears

Drain salmon. Add capers and red onion rings. Pour vinegar over mixture and toss lightly with a fork. Chill overnight.

To serve: Remove center core out of bibb lettuce. Place ½ cup of soused salmon in center. Garnish with a ripe olive, cucumber slices and asparagus spears. Makes 8 servings.

190 calories per serving
8 mg fat per serving
450 mg sodium per serving
70 mg cholesterol per serving

3-SPICE
LEMON-TUNA SALAD

grated peel of ½ lemon
2 tablespoons lemon juice
1 tablespoon honey
¼ teaspoon ground ginger
¼ teaspoon curry powder
1 - 7 oz. can tuna, drained and flaked
1½ cups seedless grapes, halved or
cantaloupe balls or cubes
½ cup celery, sliced

In large bowl combine lemon peel, lemon juice, honey, ginger, curry and garlic powder. Stir in tuna, grapes and celery; toss lightly. Serve on a bed of shredded lettuce and garnish with lemon wedges, if desired. Makes 4 servings.

A cool meal idea for a hot summer day.

---

120 calories per serving
.8 grams fat per serving
190 mg sodium per serving
30 mg cholesterol per serving

◆── HOT SEAFOOD ──◆
SALAD

1 cup white-fleshed fish or crab, cooked and flaked
1 green pepper, finely chopped
1 cup celery, finely chopped
1 small onion, finely chopped
1 cup toasted bread cubes
1 cup low fat cottage cheese
2 tablespoons mayonnaise
2 tablespoons lemon juice
1 teaspoon Worcestershire sauce
½ cup part-skim mozzarella cheese, grated
paprika

Combine all ingredients. Mix well. Pour into 1½-quart glass casserole or other baking dish. Sprinkle with paprika. Bake at 350° for 25-30 minutes.

Microwave: Cook at medium power for 10 minutes; turn once. Stir once. Makes 8 servings.

Serve this at your next luncheon.

125 calories per serving
5 grams fat per serving
220 mg sodium per serving
20 mg cholesterol per serving

LAYERED SEAFOOD SALAD

Dressing:
1 cup plain low fat yogurt
2 tablespoons mayonnaise
½ teaspoon dill weed
½ teaspoon black pepper
½ teaspoon prepared horseradish

◆

4 cups shredded lettuce
2 green onions, finely chopped
½ cup green pepper, chopped
½ cup cucumber, sliced
½ cup frozen green peas
¼ teaspoon garlic powder
2 cups cooked, flaked, white-fleshed fish, shrimp
or canned tuna
¼ cup part-skim mozzarella cheese, grated
tomato wedges

Combine all ingredients for dressing in a small bowl and set aside. Shred lettuce; add green onion, green pepper, cucumber and frozen peas. Toss lightly with garlic powder. Fill a 9x9 inch dish. Place cooked fish evenly over salad greens. Pour dressing over fish. Garnish with grated mozzarella cheese and tomato wedges. Refrigerate. Makes 4 servings.

265 calories per serving
9.7 grams fat per serving
245 mg sodium per serving
80 mg cholesterol per serving

MOLDED SEAFOOD DELIGHT

2 cups cooked, flaked, white-fleshed fish
1 - 3 oz. package lime gelatin
1 envelope plain gelatin
1½ cups boiling water
¼ cup vinegar
1 cup celery, diced
1 cup carrot, grated
¼ cup green pepper, chopped
4 green onions, finely chopped
1 cup low fat yogurt

Dissolve gelatins in boiling water. Stir in vinegar. Chill until partially set. Fold in fish, chopped vegetables and yogurt. Pour into 1½-quart ring mold. Chill until firm. Unmold onto salad greens. Garnish with sliced radishes or tomato wedges. This is an excellent salad for lunch or buffet. Makes 12 - ½ cup servings.

70 calories per serving
.4 grams fat per serving
70 mg sodium per serving
25 mg cholesterol per serving

SEAFOOD- PEAR SALAD

1 - 16 oz. can unsweetened pear halves
¼ cup low fat cottage cheese
2 tablespoons lemon juice
8 oz. imitation crab sections, broken into chunks or flakes
1 green onion, chopped
lettuce leaves

Set aside 4 pear halves. Cube remaining pear halves. In medium bowl mix cottage cheese and lemon juice. Gently fold in pear cubes, crab and green onion. Spoon into reserved pear halves. Serve on lettuce. If desired, garnish with lemon wedges and radishes. Makes 4 servings.

82 calories per serving
1.1 grams fat per serving
310 mg sodium per serving
30 mg cholesterol per serving

◆ CRAB OR ◆
SHRIMP LOUIE

lettuce leaves
2 cups lettuce leaves, shredded
1 celery stalk, sliced
radishes, sliced
2 cups cooked crab or shrimp, peeled and deveined
2 hard cooked egg whites, sliced
chives, chopped

Arrange lettuce leaves in a salad bowl. Place shredded lettuce over leaves. Add celery, radishes and seafood. Top with egg white slices and chives. Serve with Light Thousand Island Dressing on the side. Makes 4 servings.

with crab:
110 calories per serving
1.3 grams fat per serving
265 mg sodium per serving
90 mg cholesterol per serving

with shrimp:
110 calories per serving
.8 grams fat per serving
140 mg sodium per serving
160 mg cholesterol per serving

GARDEN FRESH COLESLAW

1 cup cooked shrimp, peeled and deveined
2 cups grated cabbage
2 teaspoons onion, finely chopped
½ cup green pepper, finely chopped
½ cup carrots, grated

Dressing:
½ cup plain low fat yogurt
⅛ teaspoon dry mustard
⅛ teaspoon black pepper
1 tablespoon cider vinegar
1 tablespoon sugar

Combine shrimp, cabbage, onion, green pepper and carrots and toss together. Combine ingredients for dressing and stir. Add dressing to vegetables and mix well. Serving suggestion: Serve on a bed of lettuce with tomato wedges. Makes 4 servings.

85 calories per serving
1 gram fat per serving
85 mg sodium per serving
50 mg cholesterol per serving

PICANTE SEAFOOD PASTA SALAD

1 tablespoon polyunsaturated margarine
1 cup onion, chopped
1 cup green pepper, chopped
1 cup celery, chopped
1 large clove garlic, minced
1/4 teaspoon crushed red pepper (cayenne)
2 cups tomatoes, peeled, chopped
1 bay leaf
1/2 teaspoon thyme
1/2 teaspoon oregano leaves
1/4 teaspoon rosemary leaves
1/2 teaspoon ground black pepper
1 cup tomato sauce
1/4 lb. calico or bay scallops
1/2 lb. cooked shrimp
1/2 lb. dry pasta, such as shells, gnocchi, ziti or penne

Heat margarine in non-stick skillet over medium heat. Add onion, green pepper, celery, garlic and red pepper; sauté 10 minutes or until vegetables are tender-crisp, stirring occasionally. Stir in tomatoes, bay leaf, thyme, oregano, rosemary, black pepper and tomato sauce. Simmer 15 minutes. Add scallops and shrimp; simmer just until scallops turn opaque and shrimp are hot. While sauce simmers, cook pasta in large pot of boiling water until done; drain. Combine sauce with hot pasta. Makes 6 servings.

If you can't find small bay scallops, substitute sea scallops and cut them into quarters.

275 calories per serving
2.6 grams fat per serving
560 mg sodium per serving
60 mg cholesterol per serving

EASY SHRIMP AND PEA SALAD

1 - 16 oz. package frozen peas
1 teaspoon dill weed
¼ cup red onion, chopped
1 cup cooked shrimp, peeled and deveined
2 tablespoons mayonnaise
½ cup plain low fat yogurt

Mix all ingredients together. This salad is a wonderful and easy addition to any meal. Makes 8 servings.

An easy, last minute idea for a family get-together.

100 calories per serving
3.3 grams fat per serving
70 mg sodium per serving
40 mg cholesterol per serving

◆—SHRIMP STUFFED—◆ TOMATO SALAD

¾ cup celery, diced
1½ cups cooked shrimp, peeled and deveined
¼ teaspoon pepper
2 tablespoons mayonnaise
4 ripe tomatoes
4 large lettuce leaves
1 green pepper, sliced into 4 rings
4 radishes, cut into roses
low fat yogurt, parsley sprigs and paprika to garnish

In a small mixing bowl, combine celery, shrimp, pepper and mayonnaise. Toss gently until the shrimp and celery are coated with mayonnaise. Cut each tomato into five lengthwise sections, leaving them intact at the stem end. Place each on a bed of lettuce that has been arranged on a salad plate. Spread the tomato sections apart and stuff each tomato with the shrimp salad mixture. Top each with a green pepper ring. To garnish place a spoonful of yogurt on top of each salad and garnish with a sprig of parsley and a radish rose. Sprinkle with paprika. Chill until ready to serve. Makes 4 servings.

135 calories per serving
6.3 grams fat per serving
120 mg sodium per serving
40 mg cholesterol per serving

MOLDED SHRIMP SALAD

6 oz. cooked shrimp, peeled and deveined
2 - 3 oz. packages lemon jello
2 cups hot water
1 cup cold water
2 teaspoons lemon juice
4 tablespoons celery, finely chopped
4 tablespoons green pepper, finely chopped
2 tablespoons onion, minced

Dissolve gelatin in hot water. Add cold water and lemon juice. Chill until slightly thickened. Stir in remaining ingredients. Pour into molds. Chill until firm. Makes 8 servings.

120 calories per serving
.4 grams fat per serving
85 mg sodium per serving
80 mg cholesterol per serving

SOUPS AND CHOWDERS

AUTUMN FISH STEW

1 lb. cod or haddock
1 medium onion, chopped
1 tablespoon polyunsaturated oil
1 - 28 oz. can tomatoes, undrained
2 medium potatoes, peeled and diced
½ teaspoon basil
¼ teaspoon pepper
¼ teaspoon sugar
1 - 10 oz. package frozen mixed vegetables

Cut fish fillets into bite-sized chunks. In 4-quart saucepan sauté onion in oil until tender. Stir in tomatoes with their liquid. Add potatoes, basil, pepper and sugar and cook over high heat until boiling. Reduce heat to low; cover and simmer 20-30 minutes, stirring occasionally, until potatoes are tender. Add fish and frozen mixed vegetables to tomato mixture and heat until just boiling. Reduce heat to low; cover and simmer 5 minutes or until fish flakes when tested with a fork and vegetables are tender. Makes 4 large servings.

230 calories per serving
5 grams fat per serving
370 mg sodium per serving
45 mg cholesterol per serving

HALIBUT VEGETABLE CHOWDER

"Kids Love It"

2 carrots, sliced
2 stalks celery, sliced diagonally
½ cup onion, chopped
2 cloves garlic, minced
2 tablespoons polyunsaturated oil
1 - 28 oz. can tomatoes, undrained
1 cup water
3 tablespoons parsley, minced and divided
1 teaspoon chicken bouillon granules
¼ teaspoon thyme
¼ teaspoon basil
⅛ teaspoon pepper
1½ lbs. halibut

Sauté carrots, celery, onion and garlic in oil for 5 minutes. Add undrained tomatoes, water, 2 tablespoons parsley, bouillon and seasonings. Break up tomatoes with spoon. Cover and simmer 20 minutes. Cut halibut into 1-inch cubes; add to chowder. Cover and simmer 5-10 minutes or until halibut flakes when tested with a fork. Sprinkle with remaining parsley. Makes 6 servings.

310 calories per serving
9 grams fat per serving
600 mg sodium per serving
55 mg cholesterol per serving

→ SATURDAY NIGHT → SEAFOOD CHOWDER

1 lb. salmon, fresh or frozen
3 cups water
1 small onion, diced
3 medium potatoes, unpeeled, diced
2 stalks celery, chopped
2 carrots, sliced
6-8 whole allspice
1 teaspoon dill weed
½ teaspoon white pepper
3½ cups skim milk
2 tablespoons flour
1 tablespoon polyunsaturated margarine
1 tablespoon parsley, minced

Remove skin and bones from fish. Cut fish into 1-inch chunks. Place water, onions, potatoes, celery, carrots, allspice, dill weed and white pepper into 4-quart saucepan. Cover and simmer for 15 minutes. Add 3 cups milk and salmon to vegetables. Blend flour with ½ cup skim milk until smooth. Slowly stir into chowder. Simmer for 10 minutes or until fish flakes when tested with a fork. Stir gently. Dot with margarine and parsley before serving. Serve with hot french bread. Makes 6 servings.

240 calories per serving
7 grams fat per serving
155 mg sodium per serving
50 mg cholesterol per serving

NEW ENGLAND CLAM CHOWDER

1 onion, chopped
3 stalks celery, chopped
4 medium-sized potatoes, cubed
4 carrots, sliced
1 lb. clams, minced
1½ teaspoons Italian seasoning
¼ teaspoon pepper
1 - 13 oz. can evaporated skim milk
1 tablespoon polyunsaturated margarine

Put onions, celery, potatoes, carrots, clams and spices in a 3-quart saucepan. Add water to barely cover ingredients. Cover and cook over medium heat until potatoes are tender. Add evaporated skim milk and margarine and simmer. Heat thoroughly (do not boil). Serve with a roll and salad. Makes 4 servings.

Variation: Manhattan Clam Chowder
Substitute 1 - 28 oz. can of mashed whole tomatoes for evaporated milk.

280 calories per serving
4.6 grams fat per serving
220 mg sodium per serving
45 mg cholesterol per serving

◆— GEODUCK/CLAM —◆ CHOWDER

⅔ cup onion, chopped
2 tablespoons polyunsaturated oil
12 oz. geoduck or clams, minced
½ cup boiling water
1½ cup potatoes, peeled and diced
¼ teaspoon black pepper
1 bay leaf
1 cup skim milk
1 - 13 oz. can evaporated skim milk
1 - 8½ oz. can whole kernel corn
(or 10 oz. frozen whole corn)
parsley, chopped

Sauté onion in oil in Dutch oven or 3-quart saucepan until tender but not brown. Add geoduck or clams, water, potatoes, pepper and bay leaf. Cover and simmer until potatoes are tender, about 15 minutes. Remove bay leaf. Add skim and evaporated milk and corn. Heat gently (do not boil). Garnish with parsley to serve. Makes 4 servings.

350 calories per serving
5.3 grams fat per serving
300 mg sodium per serving
30 mg cholesterol per serving

Geoduck is the largest of all American clams. Its flavor is a little richer than most clams and lends itself well to chowders.

←—ITALIAN CIOPPINO —→

1½ lbs. white-fleshed fish
1 cup onion, chopped
2 cloves garlic, minced
1 tablespoon polyunsaturated oil
1-8 oz. can tomato sauce
1-28 oz. can tomatoes, undrained and mashed
½ cup dry white wine or water
1 teaspoon each dried basil, thyme,
marjoram and oregano
1 bay leaf
¼ teaspoon pepper
4 whole cloves (optional)
1 tablespoon parsley, minced

Cut fish into ½-inch chunks and set aside. Sauté onion and garlic in oil until tender. Add tomato sauce, tomatoes, liquid and all seasonings except parsley. Let simmer 20-30 minutes, stirring occasionally. Add fish and cook until done, about 10 minutes. Add parsley. This soup is a complete meal when served with green salad and French bread. Makes about 7 cups.

Have a Cioppino party. Make base day before. Have each guest bring a quarter pound of their favorite seafood. Add to heated Cioppino base and simmer until done.

210 calories per serving
8 grams fat per serving
405 mg sodium per serving
45 mg cholesterol per serving

OYSTER STEW

1 pint container oysters, undrained
1 tablespoon polyunsaturated margarine
¼ teaspoon pepper
1 cup water
½ cup onion, finely chopped
¼ cup fresh celery leaves, chopped
1 - 13 oz. can evaporated skim milk
1 tablespoon Worcestershire sauce

Cut oysters in quarters. Melt margarine in 3-quart saucepan. Add the oysters, pepper, water, onions and celery leaves. Simmer 5 minutes. Add milk and Worcestershire sauce. Slowly heat to steaming, but do not boil. Serve hot with green salad and roll. Makes 4 servings.

Start a family tradition with oyster stew for Christmas Eve dinner.

155 calories per serving
4 grams fat per serving
215 mg sodium per serving
60 mg cholesterol per serving

FISH

◆ OVEN-POACHED ◆ ALBACORE (TUNA)

1 lb. albacore (fresh tuna), or other white-fleshed fish
1 quart water
½ cup vinegar
1 bay leaf
1 medium onion, sliced
1 carrot, diced
½ teaspoon salt (optional)

Arrange albacore in a 9x13 inch baking pan at least 2 inches deep. In a saucepan combine water, vinegar, bay leaf, onion, carrots and salt. Heat to simmering and pour over fish. Cover pan tightly with foil and put into a 400° oven for about 20 minutes, or until fish flakes with a fork. Remove from oven and carefully lift the albacore from the poaching liquid. Serve hot or chill. Poached albacore makes a fine entree or may be substituted in any recipe requiring canned tuna. Makes 4 servings.

140 calories per serving
3.5 grams fat per serving
325 mg sodium per serving
60 mg cholesterol per serving

Albacore is a premium tuna. The color of its flesh ranges from light beige to pink. The flesh turns white when cooked. Its texture is firm and flavor is mild. Albacore tuna can be baked, poached, microwaved, sauteed, broiled or grilled.

PARMESAN CATFISH

½ cup Parmesan cheese, grated
¼ cup flour
½ teaspoon pepper
1 teaspoon paprika
2 lbs. catfish fillets, skinless
3 tablespoons skim milk
2 tablespoons polyunsaturated margarine, melted

Combine Parmesan cheese, flour and seasonings. Dip catfish in milk and then coat with cheese mixture. Place in baking dish. Pour margarine over catfish and bake at 400° until golden brown and fish flakes when tested with a fork, approximately 15-20 minutes. Serve with corn bread and melon. Makes 8 servings.

190 calories per serving
8 grams fat per serving
200 mg sodium per serving
80 mg cholesterol per serving

The channel catfish is the main commercial species of the many freshwater catfish species. About 80% of the domestic catfish harvest is from Mississippi, where catfish is raised in 70,000 acre ponds. Fresh farm-raised catfish is available year-round, but the peak harvesting season is from late summer to late fall. Catfish is excellent baked, broiled, stuffed, barbecued, sauteed and steamed.

CATFISH ETTOUFFEE

1 lb. catfish, cut in large pieces, or other white-fleshed fish
¼ teaspoon pepper
dash red pepper (cayenne)
2 teaspoons polyunsaturated oil
2 cloves garlic, minced
1 tablespoon parsley, chopped
¼ large bell pepper, chopped
1 stalk celery, chopped
¼ cup green onion, chopped
1 tablespoon flour
1 – 8 oz. can tomato sauce
½ teaspoon thyme
1 bay leaf
1 slice lemon
1 tablespoon water

Select a black iron pot or saucepan that you can handle well enough to shake, as you never stir the fish while it is cooking. Rub the pieces of fish well with a mixture of black and red pepper. Put oil in the unheated pot. Arrange half of the fish on the bottom. Mix the chopped vegetables and sprinkle half over fish. Sprinkle half of flour over the vegetables and half of the tomato sauce and then repeat layers. Add the thyme, bay leaf, lemon and water. Place pot over low heat and cook slowly for one hour or until fish flakes when tested with a fork. Shake pot often to keep from sticking. Never stir as this will break the fish. When tender, taste for seasoning and add more, if necessary. Serve over rice. Makes 4 servings.

160 calories per serving
5 grams fat per serving
400 mg sodium per serving
60 mg cholesterol per serving

POACHED COD WITH HERBS

1 lb., or more as needed, cod, sea bass,
salmon steaks, or fillets
4 cups water
2 tablespoons polyunsaturated margarine
½ cup each onion, carrots and celery, chopped
2 cloves garlic, minced
6 peppercorns
3-4 whole allspice
1 teaspoon bouquet garni or fine herbs
(can be made by combining equal portions
of the following: dried dill weed, thyme, basil,
parsley, marjoram and tarragon)
2 tablespoons lemon juice

Combine ingredients, except fish, in a skillet or 3-quart saucepan and bring to a boil. Reduce heat, cover and simmer for 15-20 minutes. Place fish fillets in simmering liquid and cover until done. Remove fish with large spatula. Poached fish may be served with a squeeze of lemon or Skinny-Dip Tartar Sauce, boiled potatoes and fresh vegetables. It may also be served cold. Makes 4 servings.

Microwave: In 2-quart glass casserole, combine all ingredients except fish. Bring liquid to full boil at full power; cook additional 5 minutes. Gently place fish in poaching liquid. Cover with waxed paper. Cook at medium power. Allow 7-10 minutes for thick fillets and 3-5 minutes for thinner fillets. Do not overcook! It may be necessary to turn the thick fillets once and rearrange in dish.

white-fleshed fish:	*salmon:*
160 calories per serving	*230 calories per serving*
7.8 grams fat per serving	*15 grams fat per serving*
175 mg sodium per serving	*150 mg sodium per serving*
60 mg cholesterol per serving	*70 mg cholesterol per serving*

BASIL BAKED COD

1 lb. cod or salmon, fillets or steaks
1 tablespoon polyunsaturated margarine
1 tablespoon lemon juice
¼ teaspoon onion powder
½ teaspoon dried basil
½ bell pepper, sliced

Place fish in baking dish. Melt margarine; add lemon juice and pour over fish. Sprinkle onion powder and basil over fish. Garnish with bell pepper slices. Cover and bake in oven at 400° for 10-15 minutes or until fish flakes. Serving suggestion: Serve with baked potatoes topped with plain low fat yogurt and steamed fresh vegetables. Makes 4 servings.

white-fleshed fish:
115 calories per serving
4.4 grams fat per serving
115 mg sodium per serving
60 mg cholesterol per serving

salmon:
185 calories per serving
11 grams fat per serving
95 mg sodium per serving
70 mg cholesterol per serving

BAKED COD FILLETS

¾ cup fresh bread crumbs
3 tablespoons parsley, minced
1 teaspoon oregano
¼ teaspoon garlic powder
¼ teaspoon onion powder
⅛ teaspoon pepper
2 tablespoons polyunsaturated oil
2 lbs. cod, halibut or orange roughy fillets
1 – 16 oz. can stewed tomatoes

Combine bread crumbs, parsley and seasonings together with 1 tablespoon oil in a small mixing bowl. Spread remaining tablespoon of vegetable oil in the bottom of a 9-inch baking dish. Place fillets in baking dish. Spread bread crumb mixture evenly over the fillets. Place in 375° oven and bake for 15 minutes. Remove from oven and pour stewed tomatoes over the fillets. Return to oven and bake an additional 10-15 minutes or until fish flakes when tested with a fork. Serve with rice and steamed vegetables. Makes 6 servings.

205 calories per serving
4 grams fat per serving
270 mg sodium per serving
75 mg cholesterol per serving

CROAKER STIR-FRY

1½ lbs. croaker fillets, skinless

◆

Marinade:
3 tablespoons lemon juice,
2 tablespoons light soy sauce

◆

2 tablespoons polyunsaturated oil, divided
1 cup carrots, thinly sliced
1 cup broccoli, thinly sliced
1 cup mushrooms, sliced
¾ cup green onion, cut into ½ inch lengths
2 medium tomatoes, peeled and cut into eighths
2½ tablespoons cornstarch
¼ teaspoon pepper
1 cup cold water
reserved marinade

Cut fish into ¾-inch strips and place in bowl. Combine
lemon juice and soy sauce and pour over fish. Let marinate
while preparing vegetables. After vegetables are ready, heat
1 tablespoon oil in wok or skillet. Add carrots and stir-fry for
2 minutes. Add remaining vegetables and stir-fry for
another 2 minutes. Remove vegetables to a warm platter.
Add remaining 1 tablespoon vegetable oil to wok. Drain fish
strips; reserve marinade. Stir-fry fish strips for
approximately 2 minutes or until fish is opaque and flakes
when tested with a fork. Add vegetables to fish in wok.
Combine cornstarch, pepper, cold water and reserved
marinade; mix well. Add to fish mixture and stir only until
broth is clear and thickened. Serve over rice. Makes 6
servings.

190 calories per serving
5.7 grams fat per serving
375 mg sodium per serving
55 mg cholesterol per serving

◆— CRISPY BAKED —◆ FLOUNDER OR SOLE

1 lb. flounder or sole fillets
dash pepper
2 tablespoons polyunsaturated oil
⅓ cup cornflake crumbs

Season fillets with pepper, dip in oil and coat with cornflake crumbs. Arrange in a single layer in a lightly-oiled or shallow baking dish. Bake 10 minutes at 500° without turning or basting. Serve with green beans and boiled new potatoes, cut in quarters. Makes 4 servings.

145 calories per serving
7.5 grams fat per serving
85 mg sodium per serving
50 mg cholesterol per serving

This recipe is a tasty, light alternative to deep-fat frying.

5-SPICE HADDOCK

1 teaspoon ground cinnamon
¼ teaspoon ground nutmeg
½ teaspoon garlic powder
½ teaspoon paprika
¼ teaspoon course ground pepper
2 tablespoons polyunsaturated oil
1½ lbs. haddock fillets
1 tablespoon parsley, chopped

Combine spices in flat dish. Spread polyunsaturated oil over fillets and roll in spice mixture until coated evenly. Transfer fillets to baking dish. Bake at 450° until fish is cooked, using the 1 inch per thickness cooking method. Garnish with parsley just before serving. Makes 6 servings.

120 calories per serving
5.5 grams fat per serving
70 mg sodium per serving
80 mg cholesterol per serving

◆── BAKED STUFFED ──◆ HADDOCK

2 lbs. haddock or cod fillets, skinless

◆

Stuffing:
2 teaspoons polyunsaturated oil
¼ cup onion, chopped
¼ cup celery, chopped
2 cups bread cubes, soft
4 teaspoons parsley, chopped, divided
¼ teaspoon sage
⅛ teaspoon pepper
1 tablespoon polyunsaturated margarine, melted

Lightly oil shallow baking pan. Heat 2 teaspoons oil in small frypan. Add onion and celery. Cover and cook, stirring occasionally, until vegetables are tender. Stir in bread cubes, 3 teaspoons of parsley, sage and pepper. Arrange half of fillets in baking pan. Spread bread mixture over fillets in pan. Top with remaining fillets. Cover and bake at 400° for 15-20 minutes. Mix margarine with remaining parsley. Spoon over fish fillets. Continue baking, uncovered, until fish flakes when tested with a fork, about 5 minutes. Serve with sliced tomatoes and salad greens. Makes 8 servings.

150 calories per serving
2.5 grams fat per serving
160 mg sodium per serving
70 mg cholesterol per serving

HALIBUT IN TARRAGON

1½ lbs. halibut cheeks or steaks
½ cup lowfat yogurt
1 tablespoon mayonnaise
1 teaspoon tarragon
¾ cup part-skim mozzarella cheese, grated

Place halibut in 8x8 inch baking pan. Mix all other ingredients together and spread over halibut. Bake at 400° for 15 minutes or until fish flakes when tested with a fork. Serve with steamed carrots and cold pasta salad. Makes 6 servings.

Using our recipe guidelines, we adopted this recipe from a famous Hawaiian restaurant entree. It is wonderful for entertaining.

240 calories per serving
8.5 grams fat per serving
260 mg sodium per serving
75 mg cholesterol per serving

Halibut cheeks have been a recognized delicacy by halibut longliners for the entire duration of the North Pacific Halibut Fishery. To this day, many of the longliners remove the cheeks from the halibut before they deliver them to the processors, keeping the "best for themselves."

OVEN-FRIED HALIBUT

1½ lbs. halibut steaks
2 tablespoons polyunsaturated margarine, melted
1 tablespoon lemon juice
½ cup dry bread crumbs
½ teaspoon paprika
½ teaspoon pepper
½ teaspoon garlic powder

Cut halibut into serving-sized pieces. Melt margarine and add lemon juice. Combine bread crumbs, paprika, pepper and garlic powder. Set next to melted margarine and lemon. Dip halibut in melted margarine and lemon juice, then into crumb mixture, coating all sides. Place in single layer in lightly oiled baking dish. Bake at 450° about 10-20 minutes or until halibut flakes when tested with a fork. Serve with boiled potatoes and steamed vegetables. Makes 6 servings.

180 calories per serving
5.3 grams fat per serving
170 mg sodium per serving
5 mg cholesterol per serving

HALIBUT POT ROAST

2 lb. halibut roast, or other firm-fleshed fish,
such as salmon
12 carrots, peeled, cut lengthwise
8 medium raw potatoes, peeled and quartered
2 cups celery, sliced
1/3 cup water
1 clove garlic, minced
2 tablespoons polyunsaturated margarine, melted
1/4 teaspoon pepper

Center fish in large, lightly-oiled baking pan. Arrange vegetables around fish. Combine water and garlic; pour over fish and vegetables. Brush fish and vegetables with melted margarine. Sprinkle with pepper. Cover with foil, crimping to edges of pan. Bake at 400° for 45 minutes or until vegetables are tender and fish flakes when tested with a fork. Transfer fish and vegetables to heated serving dish. Serve with pan drippings, if desired. Makes 8 servings.

250 calories per serving
1.8 grams fat per serving
165 mg sodium per serving
55 mg cholesterol per serving

◆— HEARTY HALIBUT —◆

²/₃ cup onion, thinly sliced
2 lbs. halibut or other white-fleshed fish steaks or fillets
1¹/₂ cups mushrooms, sliced
¹/₃ cup tomatoes, chopped
¹/₄ cup green pepper, finely chopped
¹/₄ cup parsley, minced
3 tablespoons pimiento, finely chopped
¹/₂ cup white wine
2 tablespoons lemon juice
¹/₄ teaspoon dill weed
¹/₈ teaspoon pepper
lemon wedges

Arrange onion slices in the bottom of a lightly oiled baking dish and place fish on top. Combine mushrooms, tomatoes, green pepper, parsley and pimiento and spread over fish. Combine wine, lemon juice, dill weed and pepper and pour over all. Cover and bake in a 400° oven, 20 minutes, or until fish flakes when tested with a fork. Serve with lemon wedges and baked potato. Makes 8 servings.

145 calories per serving
1.4 grams fat per serving
75 mg sodium per serving
56 mg cholesterol per serving

←BAKED MACKEREL→

½ cup fresh parsley, chopped
1 teaspoon dill weed
¼ cup fresh chives, chopped
¼ cup onion, chopped
2 tablespoons lemon juice
2 lbs. dressed mackerel, or other white-fleshed fish

Mix together parsley, dill weed, chives, onion and lemon juice and sprinkle inside fish. Wrap fish in aluminum foil, sealing the edges carefully. Bake at 400° for 20-30 minutes, or until fish flakes when tested with a fork. Unwrap and remove to a hot platter; garnish with parsley and lemon slices. Makes 8 servings.

160 calories per serving
7.3 grams fat per serving
80 mg sodium per serving
40 mg cholesterol per serving

MONKFISH FINGERS
"Poor Man's Lobster"

1½ lbs. monkfish, cut into fingers to resemble
shape of lobster
(Approximately 2 inches by 1 inch)
½ cup flour
1 tablespoon polyunsaturated margarine
1 tablespoon olive oil
1 clove garlic, minced
juice from ½ of fresh lemon
¼ teaspoon fine herbs
pepper to taste
paprika

Lightly flour monkfish fingers. Melt margarine in skillet, wok or frying pan; add olive oil, garlic, lemon juice, fine herbs and pepper. Sauté monkfish fingers for about 2 minutes or until fish flakes when tested with a fork. Remove from heat. Sprinkle with paprika. Serve with boiled potatoes and steamed vegetables. Makes 6 servings.

140 calories per serving
7.4 grams fat per serving
40 mg cholesterol per serving

The monkfish is a bizaare-looking creature distinguished by its huge head, tooth-filled mouth and tiny eyes. This fish is also known as anglerfish, goosefish, bull mouth, devilfish and frogfish. Only the tail section is utilized, as the fishermen cut off and discard the enormous head and belly section. Monkfish was named when not too many years ago, only monks ate this fish. Its firm, white flesh and mild sweet flavor is highly prized. It can be baked, poached, sauteed and broiled to resemble "lobster".

LEMON BROILED OCEAN PERCH

Marinade:
juice of 1 lemon
grated peel of 1 lemon
1 tablespoon brown sugar
1 tablespoon polyunsaturated oil

◆

1 lb. ocean perch fillets
lemon wedges
parsley

To make marinade: In a baking dish combine lemon juice, lemon peel, brown sugar and oil. Mix well. Place fish in a single layer in marinade; turn to coat both sides. Cover and marinate in refrigerator for 1 hour, turning once. Lightly oil broiler pan. Transfer fish to broiler pan, reserving marinade. Baste fish with marinade during broiling. Broil 4-5 inches from source of heat for 5-7 minutes or until fish flakes when tested with a fork. Garnish with lemon wedges and parsley. Serve with rice and steamed carrots. Makes 4 servings.

130 calories per serving
4.5 grams fat per serving
70 mg sodium per serving
60 mg cholesterol per serving

←ORANGE ROUGHY→ WITH ORIENTAL SAUCE

Sauce:
1/4 cup orange juice
2 tablespoons polyunsaturated oil
2 tablespoons light soy sauce
1 tablespoon lemon juice
1 clove garlic, minced
1/8 teaspoon pepper

2 pounds orange roughy

Combine sauce ingredients. Marinate orange roughy in sauce for 15-20 minutes. Place fish on lightly oiled grill or barbeque over hot coals or broil in oven. Brush fish frequently with sauce during cooking. Makes 8 servings.

120 calories per serving
4.7 grams fat per serving
40 mg cholesterol per serving

SAUTEED ORANGE ROUGHY

2 teaspoons polyunsaturated margarine
½ cup white wine
½ teaspoon dill weed
1 garlic clove, minced
¼ cup mushrooms, chopped
½ lb. orange roughy
parsley, chopped
lemon wedges

Heat margarine, wine, dill weed, garlic and mushrooms in skillet until hot. Add fish; sauté until fish flakes when tested with a fork. Remove to a warm platter. Sprinkle with parsley. Garnish with lemon wedges. Makes 2 servings.

160 calories per serving
7 grams fat per serving
225 mg sodium per serving
50 mg cholesterol per serving

Orange roughy is imported from New Zealand. Its name comes from its brilliantly orange skin. However, the fillets are white, and have a delicate flavor.

← ORANGE ROUGHY → UNDER ORANGE SAUCE

2 lbs. orange roughy fillets
1 tablespoon polyunsaturated margarine
1 teaspoon flour
½ cup orange juice
2 teaspoons lemon juice
dash nutmeg

Cut orange roughy into 8 portions. Set aside. Melt margarine in a pan and add flour, stirring until well blended. Mix in remaining ingredients, stirring over low heat until thickened. Broil orange roughy 4 inches from heat until flesh flakes when tested with a fork. Pour orange sauce over the fish and serve immediately. Makes 8 servings.

205 calories per serving
10 grams fat per serving
85 mg sodium per serving

SPICY GRILLED ORANGE ROUGHY

Sauce:
½ cup tomato sauce
2 tablespoons green onion, minced
1 tablespoon parsley, minced
½ teaspoon Worcestershire sauce
⅛ teaspoon pepper
⅛ teaspoon basil leaves, crushed
dash sugar

1 tablespoon polyunsaturated oil
2 teaspoons lemon juice
2 lbs. orange roughy

To make sauce: Combine tomato sauce, green onion, parsley, Worcestershire sauce, pepper, basil and sugar in saucepan. Cook and stir 5 minutes over medium heat. Set aside. Mix oil and lemon juice; brush on both sides of the fish. Grill orange roughy 4 inches from coals for 5 minutes. Turn fish, baste with tomato mixture and continue cooking until orange roughy flakes when tested with a fork. Thoroughly heat remaining sauce; serve over orange roughy. This recipe may be broiled in oven. Serve with hot french bread and sliced tomatoes and cucumber. Makes 8 servings.

210 calories per serving
10 grams fat per serving
180 mg sodium per serving

HURRY UP BAKED POLLOCK
"A Meal In 20 Minutes"

1 lb. pollock fillets, or other white-fleshed fish
1 tablespoon polyunsaturated margarine, melted
1/3 cup bread crumbs
1/4 teaspoon onion powder
1/2 teaspoon dried basil
1 tablespoon lemon juice

Roll fillets in melted margarine to coat all sides. Combine bread crumbs, onion powder and basil and dredge fillets. Place coated fillets in an 8x8 inch baking dish. Sprinkle lemon juice over fish. Bake in oven at 400° for 10-15 minutes, or until fish flakes when tested with a fork. Serve with rice and steamed vegetables for a meal in 20 minutes. Makes 4 servings.

140 calories per serving
3.8 grams fat per serving
150 mg sodium per serving
50 mg cholesterol per serving

Pollock is one of the most plentiful resources in the north Pacific's fishing industry. It is an extremely lean fish with a fairly firm texture and a delicate flavor. It is marketed in 3 – 10 ounce waste-free fillets.

LEMON BAKED ROCKFISH (SNAPPER)

½ cup onion, chopped, divided in half
¾ cup fresh tomato, chopped
½ cup celery, chopped
1 lb. rockfish (snapper)
4 teaspoons Worcestershire sauce
1 tablespoon lemon juice
¼ cup parsley, chopped
lemon wedges for garnish

Combine ¼ cup of the onion with the tomato and celery. Sprinkle over bottom of an 8x8 inch baking pan. Place fish fillets over vegetables. Mix Worcestershire sauce and lemon juice; spoon over fish. Sprinkle with remaining ¼ cup onion. Bake in 400° oven about 10-15 minutes or until fish flakes when tested with a fork. Sprinkle with parsley. Serve with lemon wedges. Serve with green salad and whole wheat roll. Makes 4 servings.

130 calories per serving
2 grams fat per serving
120 mg sodium per serving
45 mg cholesterol per serving

Rockfish (Pacific Snapper) and Red Snapper are technically different species of fish. However, either may be used interchangeably in our recipes.

←BAKED ROCKFISH→ (SNAPPER) WITH CRAB

2 tablespoons polyunsaturated margarine
2 lbs. rockfish (snapper) fillets
pepper to taste
1/2 cup onion, chopped
1/2 cup white wine
1 cup canned tomatoes, undrained
3 1/2 oz. imitation crab

Melt margarine in a baking pan. Place rockfish in pan and sprinkle lightly with pepper. Add onions, white wine and tomatoes. Flake crabmeat overall and bake at 400° about 15-20 minutes or until fish flakes when tested with a fork. Makes 8 servings.

135 calories per serving
3 grams fat per serving
210 mg sodium per serving
55 mg cholesterol per serving

ROCKFISH SAUTÉ (SNAPPER)

1 lb. rockfish (snapper), skinless fillets
2 tablespoons polyunsaturated oil
1 cup carrots, thinly sliced
1 cup celery, sliced
1 cup green onion, chopped
1 cup broccoli, chopped
½ teaspoon fresh ginger, grated, or
¼ teaspoon ground ginger
¼ cup white wine
2 teaspoons cornstarch
1 teaspoon lemon peel, grated
pepper
red bell pepper, cut in strips

Remove bones from rockfish; cut into 1-inch cubes. Set aside.
Heat oil in skillet and sauté vegetables until tender-crisp.
Add fish to skillet and sauté until just begins to turn opaque.
Add ginger. Combine wine, cornstarch and lemon peel; add
to fish mixture. Cook and stir until thickened and fish flakes
when tested with a fork. Season to taste with pepper.
Garnish with red pepper. Serve with rice. Makes 4 servings.

225 calories per serving
9 grams fat per serving
100 mg sodium per serving
45 mg cholesterol per serving

OVEN POACHED ROCKFISH (SNAPPER)

4 cups skim milk
1 tablespoons polyunsaturated margarine
dash of white pepper
¼ cup green onions, chopped
1½ lbs. rockfish (snapper)

Preheat oven to 400°. Mix skim milk, margarine, white pepper and green onions in 8 × 8 inch baking pan. Cover and heat to simmering in the oven. Add snapper and cook until fish flakes when tested with a fork, approximately 10 minutes. Makes 4 servings.

300 calories per serving
10 grams fat per serving
275 mg sodium per serving
65 mg cholesterol per serving

◆ POACHED ROCKFISH ◆ (SNAPPER) WITH LEMON-TARRAGON SAUCE

1 lb. rockfish (snapper) fillets
1 quart water
¼ cup lemon juice
1 small onion, sliced
1 bay leaf
4 peppercorns
4 whole cloves

◆

Lemon-tarragon sauce:
2 tablespoons polyunsaturated margarine
1 tablespoon lemon juice
½ teaspoon tarragon
parsley, chopped

Cut rockfish into serving-sized pieces. Combine water, lemon juice, onion and seasonings. Bring to boil; simmer 20 minutes. Add rockfish. (If necessary, add boiling water to cover rockfish.) Simmer, covered, 5-10 minutes until rockfish flakes when tested with a fork. While rockfish is simmering prepare lemon-tarragon sauce: Melt 2 tablespoons margarine and add 1 tablespoon lemon juice and tarragon. Remove rockfish from water and serve on a platter with lemon-tarragon sauce poured over it; garnish with parsley. Serve with boiled new potatoes and peas. Makes 4 servings.

135 calories per serving
6.5 grams fat per serving
150 mg sodium per serving
45 mg cholesterol per serving

ROCKFISH (SNAPPER) IN FOIL

1 lb. rockfish (snapper) fillets, cut into 4 portions
2 tablespoons polyunsaturated margarine
2 tablespoons lemon juice
1/4 teaspoon pepper
1/2 cup carrots, diced
1/4 cup celery, diced
1/4 cup green onion, chopped
1 tablespoon parsley, chopped
1/2 lemon, thinly sliced

Place each fish fillet on a piece of foil about 4 inches longer than the rockfish. Melt margarine and add lemon juice, pepper, carrots, celery, onions and parsley. Pour mixture over rockfish fillets. Top with lemon slices. Bring edges of foil together and fold over several times. Twist one end to form a tail. Tuck the other end under to form a point, or nose of the fish. Place on cookie sheet and bake at 400° for 15-20 minutes or until fish flakes with a fork. Makes 4 servings.

170 calories per serving
7.3 grams fat per serving
140 mg sodium per serving
45 mg cholesterol per serving

SESAME SABLEFISH (BLACK COD)

1 lb. sablefish (black cod) fillets

◆

Marinade:
¼ cup orange juice
2 tablespoons ketchup
2 tablespoons light soy sauce
1 tablespoon lemon juice
¼ teaspoon pepper
1 teaspoon sesame oil
1 tablespoon brown sugar

Cut fish into 4 portions. Place fish in a single layer in baking dish. To make marinade: In small bowl combine orange juice, ketchup, soy sauce, lemon juice, pepper, sesame oil and brown sugar. Pour over fish. Cover and marinate in refrigerator for 2 hours, turning once. Remove fish, reserving marinade. Coat broiler pan lightly with vegetable oil; place fish on broiler pan; baste with marinade. Broil 4-5 inches from source of heat for 5-7 minutes. Turn and baste with marinade. Broil for an additional 4-5 minutes or until fish flakes when tested with a fork. Heat remaining marinade and pour over fish. Serve with rice and pineapple slices. Makes 4 servings.

190 calories per serving
7.6 grams fat per serving
545 mg sodium per serving
65 mg cholesterol per serving

Sablefish/blackcod is caught from California to Alaska by a variety of methods including longlining, potfishing and trawling. Because of its high (15-20%) oil content, sablefish has an excellent flavor and is adaptable to a number of cooking methods. A Scandinavian favorite is boiled blackcod and potatoes.

BASIC BAKED OR STEAMED SALMON

3 lb. dressed salmon
pepper
1 tablespoon polyunsaturated margarine
lemon juice
1 onion, thinly sliced

Rinse salmon. Cut head and tail off, if desired. Pepper inside and outside of salmon. Put dabs of margarine and squeeze lemon juice inside salmon cavity. Place onions inside the salmon. Wrap in foil. Bake at 400° in oven or place on rack in large pot over 2-3 inches of boiling water to steam. Cooking time is 10 minutes per pound, or about 30 minutes. Cook until fish flakes when tested with a fork. Serve with boiled potatoes and green salad. Makes 8 servings.

This method of baking or steaming can be used with any variety and size of dressed fish.

175 calories per serving
9 grams fat per serving
75 mg sodium per serving
75 mg cholesterol per serving

← BROILED SALMON → STEAKS WITH HERB SAUCE

1 lb. salmon steaks
1 tablespoon polyunsaturated margarine
¼ cup dry white wine
1 tablespoon parsley, chopped
¼ teaspoon fine herbs or bouquet garni
1 clove garlic, minced

Combine margarine, wine, parsley, herbs and garlic; heat slowly until margarine is melted. Let stand 15 minutes. Place fish on broiler pan; brush fish with sauce. Broil about 4 inches from heat source, 4-6 minutes. Turn carefully; brush with sauce. Broil 4-6 minutes longer or until fish flakes when tested with a fork. Can be barbequed instead of broiled. Serve with baked potatoes and baked squash. Makes 4 servings.

190 calories per serving
10 grams fat per serving
90 mg sodium per serving
75 mg cholesterol per serving

95

◆──── SALMON SAUTÉ ────◆

"A fifteen minute meal"

1 tablespoon polyunsaturated margaraine
¼ cup white wine
¼ cup mushrooms, sliced
8 oz. salmon fillets or steaks
lemon
parsley, chopped

Heat margarine, wine and mushrooms until hot. Place salmon in pan; sauté until done. Squeeze lemon over fish. Sprinkle with parsley before serving. Serve with pasta and steamed peas. Makes 2 servings.

225 calories per serving
13 grams fat per serving
120 mg sodium per serving
75 mg cholesterol per serving

All 5 species of salmon are equally nutritious, but vary in color, texture and cost.

Sockeye (red) — is firm in texture and deep red in color. Next to the King it is the most expensive salmon.

Pink — is your best buy. It is most often canned and has a fine texture with color ranging from light peach to deep pink.

Coho (silver) — The flesh is pink and has a fine texture. It is a moderately priced salmon.

King (Chinook) — is the most prized salmon. The King is the largest salmon, with a softer flesh that ranges from deep red to almost white. It is rich in oil.

Chum (Keta) — has coarse texture and the palest color. It is less expensive than other varieties, so it is an economical choice.

LEMON-RICE STUFFED SALMON

1 dressed salmon, about 3 lbs.
(multiply stuffing for large salmon)

◆

Stuffing:
2 tablespoons polyunsaturated margarine
1/2 cup celery, finely chopped
3/4 cup mushrooms, sliced
1/8 teaspoon thyme
1/2 teaspoon poultry seasoning
lemon pepper to taste
2/3 cup water
2 tablespoons lemon juice
3/4 cup plus 2 tablepoons precooked rice
(such as Minute Rice)
1/2 cup green onion, chopped
2-3 tablespoons pimiento, diced

◆

lemon slices
parsley

Rinse fish. Remove head and tail, if desired. Set fish aside
while preparing stuffing. Heat margarine in frying pan; add
celery and mushrooms and sauté about 5 minutes. Add
seasonings, water and lemon juice. Bring to a boil and mix in
uncooked rice. Add green onions and pimiento. Cover
stuffing; remove from heat and let stand about 5 minutes.
Pat fish dry and fill cavity with stuffing. Wrap fish in foil.
Place in a shallow baking pan. Bake in a 400° oven about
30-40 minutes, or until fish flakes when tested with a fork.
Remove upper skin and bones, if desired. Garnish with
lemon slices and parsley. Makes 8 servings.

235 calories per serving
10 grams fat per serving
100 mg sodium per serving
75 mg cholesterol per serving

SALMON IN POTATO SHELLS

1 - 15½ oz. can salmon
3 large baking potatoes
½ cup skim milk
1 teaspoon dried dill weed
1 teaspoon garlic powder
¼ teaspoon pepper
paprika

Drain salmon and flake. Bake potatoes and cool slightly. Cut in half, lengthwise, and scoop out cooked potato, leaving shell whole. Beat cooked potato with skim milk until fluffy; add more milk, if necessary. Stir in salmon, dill weed, garlic powder and pepper. Spoon into potato shells and sprinkle with paprika. Return to hot oven and bake until heated through. Makes 6 servings.

Canned salmon with bones is an excellent source of calcium.

185 calories per serving
5.2 grams fat per serving
325 mg sodium per serving
50 mg cholesterol per serving

← SALMON-STUFFED → GREEN PEPPERS

1 - 15½ oz. can salmon
6 medium green peppers
⅔ cup green onion, chopped
1½ cups cooked rice
½ cup low fat cottage cheese
2 tablespoons lemon juice
pepper to taste
1 - 15 oz. can tomato sauce

Drain salmon and flake. Cut peppers in half; remove stems, pulp and seeds. Parboil in water for 2-3 minutes or until slightly tender; invert on paper towel to drain. Mix together salmon, green onions, rice, cottage cheese, lemon juice and ½ cup of tomato sauce. Season to taste with pepper. Fill green pepper shells with salmon mixture and place in baking pan. Top with remaining tomato sauce. Bake in 400° oven for 15-20 minutes or until peppers are heated through. Serve with green salad and whole wheat roll. Makes 6 servings.

220 calories per serving
5.6 grams fat per serving
800 mg sodium per serving
50 mg cholesterol per serving

◆── SOLE AMANDINE ──◆

2 tablespoons polyunsaturated margarine, divided
1½ lbs. sole fillets
¼ cup slivered almonds, dry roasted and unsalted
1 teaspoon lemon peel, grated
2 teaspoons lemon juice
parsley
lemon wedges

In large skillet, over medium heat, melt 1 tablespoon margarine. Sauté the sole fillets for approximately 2 minutes on each side, or until fillets turn opaque. Transfer to platter and keep warm. In same skillet add remaining 1 tablespoon margarine, almonds, lemon peel and juice. Sauté 1 minute, reducing heat, if necessary, to avoid burning margarine. Pour sauce over fillets. Garnish with parsley and lemon wedges. Serve with boiled new potatoes and Garden Fresh Coleslaw. Makes 6 servings.

140 calories per serving
7 grams fat per serving
95 mg sodium per serving
45 mg cholesterol per serving

SOLE FILLETS TARRAGON

¼ cup onion, chopped
1 - 10 oz. package frozen vegetable mixture
(broccoli, cauliflower, carrots)
1 lb. sole fillets or other white-fleshed fish
pepper to taste
1 teaspoon tarragon
1 tablespoon polyunsaturated margarine
¼ cup dry white wine
lemon wedges

Combine onion and vegetables and spread over the bottom of a 8x8 inch baking dish. Place fish fillets on top of the vegetables. Sprinkle with pepper and tarragon. Dot with margarine. Pour wine over fish. Bake, covered, at 400° for 15-20 minutes or until fish flakes with a fork. To serve, lift the fish and vegetables onto a serving platter, using a slotted spoon. Garnish with lemon wedges, if desired. Serve with rice, mushrooms and peas, and frozen whole strawberries for dessert. Makes 4 servings.

180 calories per serving
6 grams fat per serving
150 mg sodium per serving
50 mg cholesterol per serving

LEMON-HERBED SOLE

1 lb. sole
pepper to taste
2 tablespoons polyunsaturated margarine, melted
1 teaspoon lemon juice
¼ teaspoon lemon peel, grated
⅛ teaspoon thyme
¼ cup white wine
1 tablespoon green onion, chopped
2 teaspoons parsley, chopped
3 tablespoons water
1 tablespoon flour
pepper
parsley sprigs
lemon wedges

Sprinkle sole with pepper. Combine melted margarine, lemon juice, lemon peel and thyme. Brush over sole; place in lightly-oiled baking dish. Sprinkle with wine, onion and parsley. Bake, covered at 400° about 12-15 minutes or until sole flakes when tested with a fork. Transfer to serving platter and keep warm. Combine water, flour and pan drippings in small saucepan. Cook and stir until thickened; pepper to taste. Top each fillet with small amount of sauce; garnish with parsley sprigs and lemon wedges. Pass remaining sauce. Makes 4 servings.

140 calories per serving
6 grams fat per serving
115 mg sodium per serving
45 mg cholesterol per serving

STUFFED SOLE WITH SHRIMP

½ lb. cooked shrimp, coarsely chopped
1 cup mushrooms, sliced
¼ green pepper, chopped
¼ cup onion, chopped
1 clove garlic, minced
⅓ cup dry bread crumbs
¼ teaspoon pepper
¼ teaspoon salt (optional)
2 tablespoons fresh parsley, chopped
½ cup Farmer's cheese
1 egg or 2 egg whites, slightly beaten
1½ lbs. sole, pollock or cod fillets
½ cup dry white wine
¼ cup lemon juice
1-2 tablespoons Farmer's cheese, grated

Preheat oven to 400°. In medium bowl, mix together shrimp, mushrooms, green pepper, onion, garlic, bread crumbs, pepper, salt, parsley and cheese. Stir in beaten egg (or whites) and mix well. Spread mixture over fillets. Roll fillets and place seam side down in 12x7½x2 inch baking dish. Pour wine and lemon juice over fish. Bake uncovered at 400° for 20-30 minutes or until fish flakes when tested with a fork. While baking, occasionally baste fillets with wine and lemon mixture. During last 5-8 minutes, sprinkle fillets with additional grated cheese. Serve with pasta. Makes 6 servings.

180 calories per serving
5 grams fat per serving
330 mg sodium per serving
(calculated without salt)
80 mg cholesterol per serving

◆— SOLE PRIMAVERA —◆ IN A SHELL

"For A Special Meal"

Marinade:
5 button-sized mushrooms, sliced
1 green onion, chopped
1/4 cup celery, diced
1/4 cup carrots, coarsely grated
1/3 cup broccoli flowerettes, chopped
1/3 cup white wine

◆

3/8 teaspoon bouquet garni
3/8 teaspoon lemon peel, finely grated
1 teaspoon dried parsley
1 clove garlic, minced
1/8 teaspoon pepper
1 1/2 tablespoons polyunsaturated margarine
3 sheets filo dough
4 ozs. sole, thinly sliced
1/4 cup flour
1/2 tablespoon Parmesan cheese
1/2 tablespoon part-skim mozzarella cheese, grated

In a covered 1-quart bowl marinate mushrooms, onion, celery, carrots and broccoli in white wine overnight. In a non-stick saucepan, simmer marinade with bouquet garni, lemon peel, parsley, garlic and pepper until tender or about 6 minutes over medium heat. Drain the cooked vegetables and set aside.

In a small pan melt margarine. On a large board or flat surface, sparingly brush one sheet of filo dough with the melted margarine. Place the second sheet of filo dough on top of the first sheet and brush sparingly with margarine; repeat the process with the third sheet of filo dough. Reserve about one teaspoon of the melted margarine.

Lightly flour sole. Place the floured sole parallel to one edge in the center of the layers of filo dough. Place well-drained, cooked vegetables on top of sole. Mix cheeses together. Sprinkle vegetables with cheese mixture. Fold ends of the filo dough to the middle overlapping one edge of dough layers by about ½-1 inch. Brush half of the reserved margarine over seam. Carefully roll the seafood and filo, beginning at the end containing fish. Brush remaining margarine over the entire roll-up. Bake at 350° for 30 minutes. Multiple recipe for as many servings as desired. Makes 1 serving.

615 calories per serving
18 grams fat per serving
370 mg sodium per serving
60 mg cholesterol per serving

TILEFISH WITH CURRY-YOGURT SAUCE

Curry-yogurt sauce:
½ cup orange low fat yogurt or
½ cup plain low fat yogurt with
1 tablespoon orange marmalade
2 teaspoons lime juice
½ teaspoon curry powder

◆

2 tablespoons polyunsaturated oil
2 tablespoons lime juice
1½ lbs. tilefish fillets or steaks, or other white-fleshed fish

To make curry-yogurt sauce: Blend together yogurt, 2 teaspoons lime juice and curry powder. Chill sauce for 15-20 minutes. Combine oil and 2 tablespoons lime juice. Baste fish with oil mixture. Place on lightly-oiled grill 5-6 inches from hot coals or broil in oven. Cook 10-15 minutes, turning once and basting frequently until fish flakes when tested with a fork. Serve with curry-yogurt sauce. Garnish with assorted fresh fruit, such as strawberries, melon and grapes. Makes 6 servings.

180 calories per serving
4.5 grams fat per serving
90 mg sodium per serving
80 mg cholesterol per serving

Tilefish is found along the outer edge of the continental shelf from Nova Scotia to Florida and the Gulf of Mexico. Tilefish can grow to over 40 pounds, but most weigh from 4-7 pounds. The lean, white flesh is often compared to lobster or scallop meat. The tilefish diet, primarily red crab and other shellfish is reflected in its flavor.

HUKE LODGE BREAKFAST TROUT

2 tablespoons brown sugar
¼ teaspoon salt
2 tablespoons polyunsaturated margarine
4 whole gutted trout (approximately 1½ lbs.)

Remove heads of trout, if desired. Place sugar and salt in a heavy cast-iron pan covered with a lid and slightly burn over heat. Add the margarine and trout; cover and cook trout over low heat for about 5-10 minutes on each side, or until fish flakes when tested with a fork. The trout will have a delicious smokey flavor. Serve with hash browned potatoes and fresh fruit. Makes 4 servings.

270 calories per serving
16.9 grams fat per serving
255 mg sodium per serving
50 mg cholesterol per serving

SHELLFISH

CLAMS MOZZARELLA

1½ lbs. frozen chopped clams, thawed and drained
2 tablespoons fresh parsley, finely chopped
2 tablespoons chives, chopped
2 cloves garlic, finely minced
dash red pepper (cayenne)
dash black pepper
12 oz. part-skim mozzarella cheese, shredded
6 slices pumpernickel bread

Sauté clams with parsley, chives, garlic and peppers in pan for 2-3 minutes. Spoon clam mixture into a bowl and toss with mozzarella cheese. Line 9x13 inch pan with bread, and spoon clam and cheese mixture evenly over bread. Broil until golden brown and bubbly. Cut into serving-sized pieces. Serve immediately. This makes a wonderful lunch entree or can be served at buffets or potluck dinners. It also makes a wonderful appetizer. For individual appetizers, spread clam and cheese mixture over snack-sized bread slices and heat under broiler. Makes 6 servings.

290 calories per serving
2.3 grams fat per serving
530 mg sodium per serving
360 mg cholesterol per serving

◆— CRAB ST. JACQUES —➔

½ cup mushrooms, sliced
2 tablespoons onion, finely minced
1 tablespoon polyunsaturated margarine
2 teaspoons cornstarch
½ cup skim milk
1 tablespoon dry white wine
1 tablespoon lemon juice
¼ teaspoon thyme
⅛ teaspoon white pepper
8 oz. crab meat (imitation crab may be used)
bread crumbs
1 oz. part-skim mozzarella cheese, grated

Sauté mushrooms and onions in margarine. Blend in cornstarch. Add milk, wine and lemon juice. Cook on medium heat, stirring constantly, until thickened and smooth. Blend in seasonings. Add crab and heat through. Divide between 2 scallop shells or individual au gratin dishes. Sprinkle bread crumbs and mozzarella cheese over casseroles. Broil 3 to 5 inches from heat, 3 to 4 minutes or until lightly browned. Serve with fruit plate and whole wheat roll. Makes 2 servings.

280 calories per serving
10 grams fat per serving
410 mg sodium per serving
80 mg cholesterol per serving

112

CRAB BROCCOLI CASSEROLE

1 - 10 oz. package frozen broccoli spears
2 tablespoons polyunsaturated margarine
2 tablespoons flour
1 cup skim milk
dash pepper
dash paprika
6 oz. cooked crab meat (imitation crab may be used)
¼ cup green onion, thinly sliced
1 tablespoon pimiento, coarsely chopped
2 tablespoons slivered almonds, dry roasted, unsalted

Thaw broccoli and cut stems in bite-sized pieces, keeping flowerettes separate. Make a white sauce by melting margarine in small saucepan; slowly stir in flour, then skim milk. Cook over moderate heat until thickened, stirring constantly. Fold in crab meat, onion and pimiento. Arrange broccoli flowerettes around edge of a 8x8 inch baking dish. Fill center with remaining broccoli pieces and spoon sauce over broccoli in center of casserole. Sprinkle nuts over top. Bake in 375° oven for 20 minutes or until hot and bubbly. Serve with fruit salad and whole wheat bread. Makes 4 servings.

Make this entree ahead of time and refrigerate.
Add 5 to 10 minutes to cooking time.

160 calories per serving
6.7 grams fat per serving
240 mg sodium per serving
45 mg cholesterol per serving

CRAB WITH RED SAUCE

1 tablespoon polyunsaturated margarine
2 tablespoons onion, minced
1 clove garlic, minced
8 oz. can tomato sauce
¼ cup ketchup
¼ teaspoon oregano, crushed
1½ lbs. cooked crab meat, thawed if necessary
(imitation crab may be used)

Melt margarine in skillet. Add onion and garlic and sauté until tender; stir in remaining ingredients. Simmer 5 minutes. Serve over fettucine noodles. Makes 6 servings.

130 calories per serving
3.2 grams fat per serving
620 mg sodium per serving
90 mg cholesterol per serving

◆── IMITATION CRAB ──➤ LEG OR SCALLOP SAUTÉ

1 lb. imitation crab legs or scallops
2 tablespoons flour
2 tablespoons polyunsaturated margarine
¼ cup green onion, minced
1 clove garlic, minced
½ cup mushrooms, thinly sliced
¼ cup sherry
pepper to taste
parsley

Dust crab legs or scallops very lightly with flour. In a large frying pan heat margarine. Add onions, garlic and mushrooms. Sauté until the mushrooms are tender. Add crab legs or scallops and sherry; cook at a very high heat, until sherry is reduced by half. When finished, there should be only a very light brown sauce glazing the crab legs or scallops. Pepper to taste. Serve with rice sprinkled with parsley and a green salad. Makes 4 servings.

150 calories per serving
6.5 grams fat per serving
660 mg sodium per serving
90 mg cholesterol per serving

Imitiation crab and other similar products are made from natural seafood. These products are made from white fish, usually Pacific pollock, which is deboned, minced and washed, and reduced to a paste, called surimi. Meat or juices of crab, shrimp or scallops may be mixed in to the surimi. It is then shaped to resemble shrimp, scallops and crab legs or flakes. Their use is common in some restaurants, in dishes such as seafood salads. The popularity of these imitation products is growing among cost-conscious consumers, who find the taste and texture agreeable.

←─ BROILED OYSTERS ─→

1 lb. oysters, shucked – 12 large or 20 medium or 30 small
2 tablespoons polyunsaturated margarine
1 teaspoon dill weed
lemon wedges

Shuck, drain and dry oysters on a paper towel. Place them on a baking sheet. Melt margarine; add dill and brush over oysters. Broil about 3 minutes, until lightly browned, turning once. Serve with "Zesty Cocktail Sauce" and lemon wedges. Makes 4 servings.

130 calories per serving
6.8 grams fat per serving
155 mg sodium per serving
60 mg cholesterol per serving

Oysters are an excellent source of iron and zinc.

◆——— BROILED ———◆
SCALLOP SAUTERNE

1 lb. scallops or imitation scallops
1 tablespoon lemon juice
1 teaspoon thyme
½ teaspoon dill weed
2 tablespoons sauterne
2 teaspoons parsley, chopped
lemon wedges

Sprinkle scallops with lemon juice, thyme, dill weed and sauterne in a bowl. Toss lightly. Place on broiler pan. Broil 3-4 minutes. Sprinkle with parsley and serve with lemon wedges. Makes 4 servings.

97 calories per serving
2.5 grams fat per serving
290 mg sodium per serving
55 mg cholesterol per serving

All scallops are the same biologically, but vary in size.
They are grouped into three categories based on size:
Sea scallops – 10-40 per pound
Bay scallops – 40-100 per pound
Calico scallops – over 100 per pound

OYSTER OR SCALLOP SAUTÉ

2 tablespoons polyunsaturated margarine
½ cup white wine
⅓ cup celery, chopped
2 cups mushrooms, sliced
½ cup green onions, chopped
½ cup red or green pepper, chopped
1½ lbs. scallops or oysters
1 teaspoon dill weed
parsley, chopped
squeeze of lemon

Sauté margarine, wine and vegetables in a saucepan until tender-crisp. Add scallops and dill weed and sauté in pan, until scallops are opaque. Sprinkle with parsley and squeeze of lemon. Serve with bulger and orange slices. Makes 6 servings.

160 calories per serving
4 grams fat per serving
350 mg sodium per serving
55 mg cholesterol per serving

BROILED SHELLFISH

1 lb. scallops or
1 lb. raw prawns, shrimp or crayfish,
shelled and deveined or
1 lb. oysters
2 tablespoons polyunsaturated margarine, melted
1 tablespoon lemon juice
¼ teaspoon paprika
¼ teaspoon garlic powder
parsley, chopped

Arrange shellfish over bottom of a heat-proof dish. Combine remaining ingredients except parsley. Spoon half of mixture over shellfish. Broil 3 inches from heat, allowing 3-6 minutes for scallops, prawns, shrimp, crayfish or oysters. Baste occasionally with remaining mixture. Sprinkle with parsley before serving. Makes 4 servings.

Variation: Shellfish kabobs
Substitute polyunsaturated oil for margarine and marinate scallops, prawns, crayfish, shrimp or oysters in basting mixture for ½ hour. Arrange on skewers alternately with choice of mushrooms, pineapple chunks, par-boiled green pepper squares or small cooked onions. Broil as above, allowing 5-7 minutes on each side. Baste occasionally with remaining marinade mixture. Makes 4 servings.

160 calories per serving
6.4 grams fat per serving
225 mg sodium per serving
180 mg cholesterol per serving

◆—SESAME PRAWNS—◆

"Wonderful"

1 tablespoon polyunsaturated margarine
1 tablespoon light soy sauce
½ lb. prawns or shrimp, peeled and deveined
1 tablespoon sesame seeds
¼ cup green onion, diagonally sliced
¼ teaspoon ground ginger or
1 teaspoon fresh ginger, grated

Heat margarine in frying pan or wok. Add soy sauce, prawns or shrimp and sesame seeds. Cook over medium heat until shellfish is opaque, approximately 2-3 minutes. Stir in green onion and ginger; heat thoroughly. Serve over wild rice. Makes 2 servings.

195 calories per serving
10 grams fat per serving
515 mg sodium per serving
160 mg cholesterol per serving

There are numerous varieties of shrimp or prawns. Size ranges from 3-160 to the pound. The interchange in names "shrimp" or "prawn" has no universal standard. However, in commercial practice in the U.S., prawn is used as a name for large shrimp.

← POACHED PRAWNS →

1 quart water
1 small lemon, sliced or 2 tablespoons lemon juice
1 small onion, sliced
2 teaspoons pickling spices
¼ teaspoon salt (optional)
1½ lbs. raw prawns or shrimp

Combine water with lemon, onion and spices. Bring to boil and add prawns. Cover and simmer 3 minutes. Drain and cool. Remove shells and devein. Use in recipe calling for cooked prawns or shrimp. Makes 4 servings.

165 calories per serving
1.4 grams fat per serving
235 mg sodium per serving (calculated without salt)
265 mg cholesterol per serving

Variation: Prawns in Beer

3 cups beer
1 cup water
1 bay leaf
1½ lbs. raw prawns or shrimp

Bring beer, water and bay leaf to boil. Add prawns. Cover and simmer 5 minutes. Drain. Remove shells and devein. Serve warm or chilled. Makes 4 servings.

180 calories per serving
1.4 grams fat per serving
240 mg sodium per serving (calculated without salt)
265 mg cholesterol per serving

◄— ALMOND SHRIMP —► AND PEPPERS

Marinade:
2 tablespoons lemon juice
3 cloves garlic, finely minced
1/8 teaspoon red pepper (cayenne)
1/2 teaspoon black pepper
1 tablespoon olive oil
2 tablespoons chives, thinly sliced, or
2 teaspoons dried chives
2 tablespoons parsley, chopped
2 teaspoons dried basil

1 1/2 lbs. medium, raw shrimp or crayfish,
peeled and deveined
1 red bell pepper, julienne cut
1/2 cup blanched slivered almonds
1 tablespoon polyunsaturated margarine
lemon wedges

To make marinade: Combine lemon juice, garlic, red pepper (cayenne), black pepper, olive oil, chives, parsley and basil. Add shellfish and marinate 15 minutes at room temperature. In wok or skillet sauté bell pepper and almonds in margarine, until bell pepper is tender-crisp. Add marinade with seafood and continue sauteing for 2-3 minutes or until shellfish is opaque. Garnish with lemon wedges. Serve with grape clusters and rice. Makes 6 servings.

160 calories per serving
10 grams fat per serving
180 mg sodium per serving
180 mg cholesterol per serving

◆ GINGERED SHRIMP ◆ ON SKEWERS

Marinade:
2 tablespoons lemon juice
2 tablespoons sesame oil
2 tablespoons green onion, minced
1 teaspoon fresh ginger or
¼ teaspoon ground ginger

1 lb. (about 40) medium-sized shrimp,
peeled and deveined
8 crisp romaine lettuce leaves
lemon wedges
1 large cucumber, cut into ¼-inch thick slices

To make marinade: In a bowl or a double plastic bag combine lemon juice, sesame oil, green onion and ginger. Place shrimp in bowl or bag and marinate for 30 minutes at room temperature. Remove shrimp from marinade and place on skewers. Broil 2-3 minutes. Garnish plate with lettuce leaves and lemon wedges. Arrange cucumber slices on lettuce leaves and place skewered shrimp on plate. Serve with rice. Makes 4 servings.

170 calories per serving
7.9 grams fat per serving
160 mg sodium per serving
180 mg cholesterol per serving

LUNCHTIME PICNIC BARBECUE

SALMON IN PITA BREAD

1 - 7¾ oz. can salmon, drained
¼ cup garbanzo beans, coarsely chopped
¼ cup celery, chopped
2 tablespoons onion, chopped
1 tablespoon parsley, chopped
¼ cup low fat yogurt
dash pepper
dash oregano
lettuce, shredded
2 pita bread, halved
1 tomato, cut into wedges

Drain salmon and break into large chunks. Combine with beans, celery, onion and parsley. Combine yogurt, pepper and oregano; gently toss with salmon mixture. Place lettuce in pita bread halves, distribute salmon mixture evenly over lettuce. Garnish with tomato wedges. Makes 4 servings.

200 calories per serving
6 grams fat per serving
435 mg sodium per serving
30 mg cholesterol per serving

— TAKE-ME-ALONG —
SEAFOOD SANDWICH

1 - 7¾ oz. can salmon or
1 - 7 oz. can tuna, drained
2 tablespoons low fat cottage cheese
1 tablespoon mayonnaise
1 tablespoon sunflower seeds, unsalted, dry roasted
1 tablespoon unsweetened pineapple,
crushed, fresh or canned
1 tablespoon celery, finely chopped
tomato slices
cucumber slices
alfalfa sprouts

Combine fish with remaining ingredients and mix. Use as a sandwich spread with tomato, cucumber slices and alfalfa sprouts on 1 slice whole grain bread or in pita bread. Serving suggestions: Serve with fresh fruit salad. Serve as a cool and crunchy seafood salad on a bed of shredded lettuce. Makes 4 open-faced sandwiches.

with salmon:	*with tuna:*
200 calories per sandwich	*165 calories per sandwich*
7.7 grams fat per sandwich	*5.3 grams fat per sandwich*
405 mg sodium per sandwich	*315 mg sodium per sandwich*
40 mg cholesterol per sandwich	*35 mg cholesterol per sandwich*

DANISH SANDWICHES

1 - 7¾ oz. can salmon, drained
2 tablespoons celery, chopped
2 tablespoons green onion, finely chopped
2 tablespoons mayonnaise
2 teaspoons lemon juice
dash of pepper
¼ teaspoon dill weed
6 slices whole wheat bread
bibb lettuce
cucumber, thinly sliced
radish, thinly sliced
parsley sprigs

Flake salmon. Combine salmon, celery, green onion, mayonnaise, lemon juice, pepper and dill weed. Place a leaf of lettuce on each slice of bread. Overlap cucumber and radish slices on each sandwich. Mound salmon mixture in center. Garnish with parsley sprigs. Makes 6 servings.

155 calories per serving
7.5 grams fat per serving
345 mg sodium per serving
20 mg cholesterol per serving

TUNA-COTTAGE CHEESE SANDWICH

¼ cup low fat cottage cheese
1 - 7 oz. can tuna, drained and flaked
(salmon may be substituted)
1 tablespoon mayonnaise
¼ cup celery, finely chopped
2 tablespoons green onion, minced
5 radishes, diced
pepper to taste
2 tablespoons slivered almonds
3 English muffins, split and toasted

Combine all ingredients. Spread on 6 muffin halves. Serve with tomato wedges. Makes 6 sandwiches.

160 calories per sandwich
3.5 grams fat per sandwich
245 mg sodium per sandwich
20 mg cholesterol per sandwich

ENGLISH MUFFIN SHRIMP PIZZA

"A Teenage Favorite"

6 English muffins, split

Pizza Sauce:
1 - 15 oz. can tomato sauce
1½ teaspoons Italian seasoning
1 tablespoon dry parsley flakes
½ teaspoon garlic powder
½ teaspoon onion powder
¼ teaspoon pepper

¾ cup onion, chopped
¾ cup mushrooms, sliced
¾ cup green pepper, chopped
½ lb. cooked shrimp (2 cups), peeled and deveined
4 oz. part-skim mozzarella cheese, shredded

Toast English muffins. Mix ingredients for pizza sauce.
Place pizza sauce on muffins. Top with onions, mushrooms
and green pepper. Add shrimp. Cover with shredded cheese.
Broil pizza about 3 minutes or until cheese melts. Makes 12
individual pizzas.

130 calories per pizza
3.8 grams fat per pizza
400 mg sodium per pizza
30 mg cholesterol per pizza

BARBECUED CATFISH

2 lbs. catfish fillets, skinless

◆

Sauce:
2 tablespoons polyunsaturated oil
1/3 cup lemon juice
1/4 cup onion, chopped
2 tablespoons ketchup
2 teaspoons Worcestershire sauce
4 bay leaves, crushed
2 cloves garlic, minced
1/4 teaspoon pepper
2 teaspoons sugar

◆

paprika

Place fish in a single layer in a shallow baking dish. To make sauce: Combine remaining ingredients, except paprika. Pour sauce over fillets and let stand for 30 minutes, turning once. Remove fillets, reserving sauce for basting. Place fillets on lightly-oiled wire grill. Sprinkle with paprika. Cook about 4 inches from moderately hot coals for 5 minutes. Baste with sauce and sprinkle with paprika. Turn and cook for 5-10 minutes longer, or until fish flakes when tested with a fork. Recipe may be broiled in oven. Serve with corn on the cob and fresh fruit. Makes 8 servings.

160 calories per serving
7 grams fat per serving
120 mg sodium per serving
60 mg cholesterol per serving

THYMELY MARINATED LINGCOD

"Simple, But Delicious"

½ cup onion, chopped
2 tablespoons polyunsaturated oil
½ teaspoon thyme
½ teaspoon oregano
½ teaspoon rosemary
½ teaspoon pepper
¼ teaspoon salt (optional)
½ cup lemon juice
1 clove garlic, minced

2 lbs. lingcod or other whitefleshed fish

Combine all ingredients and marinate lingcod for 30 minutes. Broil or barbeque until fish flakes. Makes 8 servings.

115 calories per serving
4.3 grams fat per serving
82 mg sodium per serving
(calculated without salt)
90 mg cholesterol per serving

BARBECUED SALMON

1 lb. salmon steaks or fillets
Snappy barbecue sauce
or
Barbecue basting sauce

Place 1 lb. salmon steaks or fillets in a tray made of heavy duty foil with 1-inch sides. Place on grill about 10-12 inches over hot charcoals. Cook for 5-20 minutes until fish flakes. (Time of cooking varies based on the type, cut and thickness of the fish.) Be careful not to overcook. The fish may be basted during the last 2-3 minutes of cooking with about ½ cup "Snappy Barbecue Sauce" or "Barbecue Basting Sauce". Basting will keep the fish moist.
Serving suggestion: Serve with salad, whole grain rolls, fresh vegetables and fruit. Hint: For extra moist fish, place foil lightly over top of seafood during cooking. Makes 4 servings.

Kick off your fourth of July picnic with barbequed salmon. Salmon supplies are plentiful during summer and fall.

White-fleshed fish:
90 calaries per serving
.9 grams fat per serving
80 mg sodium per serving
60 mg cholesterol per serving

Salmon:
160 calories per serving
7.7 grams fat per serving
60 mg sodium per serving
70 mg cholesterol per serving

←SALMONBURGERS→

1 - 15½ oz. can salmon
1 egg
½ cup onion, chopped
1 tablespoon parsley, chopped
1 tablespoon lemon juice
1 teaspoon Worcestershire sauce
¾ cup oats, quick cooking
dash pepper

Drain salmon; combine with all other ingredients. Form into 4 patties. Use a lightly-oiled non-stick skillet and pan fry until golden brown on both sides. Place salmon patties on bottom half of hamburger bun. Serve with lettuce, sliced tomato and pickles. For barbecuing, cook on lightly-oiled piece of foil for 6 minutes; turn and cook 6 minutes longer. Makes 4 servings.

Salmonburgers are a creative alternative to hamburgers. Try this recipe at a summer barbecue.

300 calories per serving
11 grams fat per serving
490 mg sodium per serving
130 mg cholesterol per serving

SOLE WITH VEGETABLES IN FOIL

1 lb. sole or flounder fillets, cut into 4 portions
1 lemon, sliced
1 medium carrot, julienne cut
¼ lb. fresh pea pods, stem ends and strings removed
8 green onions, julienne cut
2 tablespoons polyunsaturated margarine
1 teaspoon fine herbs or bouquet garni
18 inch-wide heavy-duty foil

Tear off 4 - 12 inch long sheets of foil. Place fish fillet in center of each piece of foil. On each fish fillet place 2 lemon slices and ¼ of the carrots, pea pods and green onions; dot with margarine and sprinkle with fine herbs. For each packet, bring sides of foil together over fish. Place packets on cookie sheet. Bake fish at 400° for 10-20 minutes or until fish flakes when tested with a fork. Transfer to serving plates. Serve directly from packets. Serve with Garden Fresh Coleslaw and bread sticks. Makes 4 servings.

Prepackage before you go to work. When you come home, head to the beach for an open-pit barbecue.

180 calories per serving
6.7 grams fat per serving
160 mg sodium per serving
50 mg cholesterol per serving

SWORDFISH KABOBS

1 lb. swordfish, or other firm white-fleshed fish
cut into 1" chunks
1 - 20 oz. can unsweetened pineapple chunks,
reserve 3 tablespoons of juice

Marinade:
2 tablespoons light soy sauce
2 tablespoons sherry
2 teaspoons fresh ginger, grated
½ teaspoon dry mustard
2 cloves garlic, minced
1 teaspoon brown sugar
2 tablespoons polyunsaturated oil

1-2 large green peppers, par-boiled, cut into large pieces

Place swordfish chunks in marinade pan. Drain pineapple and reserve 3 tablespoons juice. Set pineapple chunks aside. Make marinade by combining reserved juice, soy sauce, sherry, ginger, mustard, garlic, brown sugar and oil. Stir well and pour over swordfish. Cover and marinate in refrigerator for 1 hour, turning once. Using bamboo or metal skewers, make kabobs by alternating pineapple, green pepper and swordfish; set aside. Place on lightly oiled grill 4-5 inches from hot coals and cook 4-5 minutes or until swordfish flakes when tested with a fork. The kabobs may be broiled in the oven. Serve with pasta salad and fresh fruit. Makes 4 servings.

Let guests at dinner be creative and helpful, by making their own kabobs.

300 calories per serving
11.5 grams fat per serving
450 mg sodium per serving
50 mg cholesterol per serving

TURBOT FILLET & PINEAPPLE IN FOIL

1½ lbs. turbot fillets, or other white-fleshed fish
¼ teaspoon pepper
¼ teaspoon ginger
1 - 20 oz. can unsweetened pineapple chunks, drained
1 green pepper, cut in 24 strips
6 tomato slices

Cut fillets into 6 portions. Season fillets. Cut 6-12 inch squares of aluminum foil. On each square place fillet portion, 6 pineapple chunks, 4 strips of green pepper and 1 slice of tomato. Seal the foil with a double fold making it steamtight. Place packages in shallow baking pan. Bake at 400° for 20-30 minutes or until fish flakes with a fork. Makes 6 servings.

This recipe is fun for a beach or at-home barbecue. Make ahead of time and have the kids help!

200 calories per serving
8 grams fat per serving
90 mg sodium per serving

◆— SLIPPER LOBSTER —◆ TAIL KABOBS

12 slipper lobster tails
fresh vegetables of your choice, such as
cherry tomatoes, green pepper, zucchini, onion,
mushrooms, cut into 2-inch cubes
4 skewers
Barbecue Basting Sauce

Remove lobster meat from shells. Thread skewers, alternating lobster with vegetables. These can be assembled ahead of time and refrigerated until placing on the grill or barbecue. Baste while cooking with Barbecue Basting Sauce. Serve hot. Makes 4 servings.

Soak bamboo skewers in water for ½ hour to prevent them from burning on the grill.

---

175 calories per serving
2.7 grams fat per serving
325 mg sodium per serving
90 mg cholesterol per serving

◆——— BARBECUED ——◆ OYSTERS IN THE SHELL

Oysters in shell
12 large or 20 medium or 32 small

Scrub oyster shells thoroughly. Place oysters on a barbecue grill, lid side up*, about 4 inches from hot coals. Barbecue 5-10 minutes or until shells begin to open. (The larger the oyster, the longer the cooking time.) Some oysters may need a gentle nudge to open. Place a knife under the lid of the oyster and pry the shells apart. "Snappy Barbecue Sauce" or "Barbecue Basting Sauce" may be served with the oyster. Makes 4 servings.

90 calories per serving
2.5 grams fat per serving
90 mg sodium per serving
45 mg cholesterol per serving

*Oysters in the shell have two sides. The lid of the oyster is flat. The cup of the oyster is bowl shaped. In order to retain the juice in the oyster, be sure to place oysters on the grill with the lid side up.

MICROWAVE

Seafood cooked in a microwave oven is excellent. Microwave cooking of seafood utilizes their natural moisture and retains juices.

For best results in cooking seafood in a microwave, follow these instructions:

1. Microwave individual portions on High setting to retain juices and flavor.
2. Do not overcook seafood.
3. Keep thicker edges and large pieces of fish toward the outside of the cooking container.
4. Cover the container while cooking, so the center will be done and the edges will stay moist.
5. Let seafood stand 2-3 minutes prior to serving.

SPANISH STYLE COD

½ lb. cod fillets
pepper
⅓ cup onion, chopped
3 tablespoons green chiles, diced
1 tablespoon polyunsaturated oil
1 tomato, chopped
¼ cup parsley, chopped
1 tablespoon lime juice
¼ teaspoon oregano leaves
dash sugar
4 green pepper rings
lime wedges

Oven method:
Sprinkle cod with pepper. Sauté onion and chiles in oil. Add tomato, parsley, lime juice, oregano and sugar. Arrange green pepper rings on fillets in baking dish. Pour tomato mixture over fish. Bake at 400° for 10 minutes or until fish flakes when tested with a fork. Serve with rice; garnish with lime wedges. Makes 2 servings.

Microwave method:
Sprinkle cod with pepper. Combine onion, chiles, oil, tomato, parsley, lime juice, oregano and sugar. Arrange green pepper rings on fillets in microwave-proof baking dish. Pour tomato mixture over fish; cover with plastic wrap. Microwave at HIGH 3 minutes. Rotate dish ¼ turn; microwave at HIGH 3-4 minutes longer, or until cod flakes when tested with a fork.

200 calories per serving
8 grams fat per serving
100 mg sodium per serving
50 mg cholesterol per serving

◆ QUICK & EASY ◆
MICROWAVE POACHED
FLOUNDER

1 lb. flounder fillets
½ cup white wine
⅛ teaspoon pepper

Place fish fillets in microwave dish. Pour wine over fish fillets. Sprinkle with pepper. Cover with plastic wrap. Microwave at medium power until fish flakes when tested with a fork, about 5-10 minutes or follow manufacturer's instructions. Serve with microwaved potatoes and vegetables. Makes 4 servings.

Try this recipe in a microwavable plastic bag.

115 calories per serving
1 gram fat per serving
80 mg sodium per serving
55 mg cholesterol per serving

The myth that seafood from saltwater is high in salt or sodium is not true. Fresh or frozen seafood without breading or sauce is moderately low in sodium.

AFTER WORK GROUPER (CHILEAN SEA BASS)

1 lb. grouper
1½ tablespoons polyunsaturated margarine, melted
¼ cup dry bread crumbs
1 tablespoon parsley, chopped
⅛ teaspoon pepper
⅛ teaspoon paprika
lemon wedges

Microwave method:
Cut grouper into serving-sized pieces. Coat on all sides with margarine. Place in microwave-proof dish. Combine bread crumbs, parsley and seasonings. Sprinkle crumb mixture over grouper. Cover with plastic wrap; microwave at HIGH 2 minutes. Rotate dish ¼ turn; microwave at HIGH 1-2 minutes longer or until grouper flakes when tested with a fork. Serve with lemon wedges. Makes 4 servings.

Oven method:
Cut grouper into serving-sized pieces. Coat on all sides with melted margarine. Place on broiling pan. Combine bread crumbs, parsley and seasonings. Dip grouper in crumb mixture. Broil for 10 minutes or until grouper flakes when tested with a fork. Serve with lemon wedges. Makes 4 servings.

160 calories per serving
4.7 grams fat per serving
145 mg sodium per serving

Grouper inhabit temperate and tropical waters throughout the world. About 70 species are found in U.S. waters, primarily along the Gulf Coast and Atlantic states. Other names for grouper include Chilean sea bass, jewfish, black grouper, yellowmouth grouper and red grouper. The largest grouper can weigh in excess of 600 pounds. The white flesh is ideal for poaching, steaming, broiling and barbecuing.

◆——— CITRUS-BAKED ———◆ HADDOCK OR COD

½ lb. haddock or cod fillets
pepper
1 tablespoon lemon juice
1 teaspoon polyunsaturated oil
½ medium onion, sliced in thin rings
1 small orange, peeled and sliced
2 teaspoons parsley, minced

Oven method:
Sprinkle cod or haddock with pepper. Combine lemon juice and oil; brush on all sides of fish. Place fish in baking dish and arrange onion rings over fish; brush with remaining lemon-oil mixture. Bake at 400° for 5 minutes. Arrange orange slices over onion; sprinkle with parsley. Bake 5 to 8 minutes longer or until fish flakes when tested with a fork. Makes 2 servings.

Microwave Method:
Sprinkle cod or haddock with pepper. Combine lemon juice and oil in microwave-proof baking dish; turn fish to coat all sides with lemon-oil mixture. Arrange onion slices over fish. Cover with plastic wrap; microwave at HIGH 2 minutes. Remove cover and arrange orange slices over onion; sprinkle with parsley and cover. Rotate dish ¼ turn; microwave at HIGH 2 to 3 minutes longer or until fish flakes when tested with a fork. Makes 2 servings.

130 calories per serving
4.5 grams fat per serving
60 mg sodium per serving
60 mg cholesterol per serving

CANTONESE-STYLE LINGCOD

1 lb. lingcod fillets
1 tablespoon polyunsaturated margarine
2 teaspoons lemon juice
pepper

◆

Sauce:
1 tablespoon packed brown sugar
2 teaspoons cornstarch
2 tablespoons each water and cider vinegar
1 tablespoon light soy sauce
1 cup celery, diagonally sliced
½ cup canned unsweetened pineapple chunks, drained

Microwave method:
Cut cod into serving-sized pieces; place in microwave-proof dish. Dot with margarine; sprinkle with lemon juice. Season with pepper. Cover with waxed paper; microwave at HIGH 2 minutes. Rotate dish ¼ turn; microwave at HIGH 1-2 minutes longer or until cod flakes when tested with a fork. Remove from microwave oven and keep cod covered while preparing sauce. To make sauce: Combine brown sugar and cornstarch in 4-cup glass measure; add cold water, vinegar and soy sauce. Microwave at HIGH 1 minute or until thickened. Stir once during cooking. Stir in celery and pineapple. Microwave at HIGH 2 minutes. Serve over cod with rice. Makes 4 servings.

continued on next page

Oven method:
Cut cod into serving-sized pieces; place in shallow baking dish. Dot with margarine; sprinkle with lemon juice. Season with pepper. Bake at 400° for 10 minutes, or until cod flakes when tested with a fork. While cod is cooking, make sauce. To make sauce: Combine brown sugar, cornstarch, cold water, vinegar and soy sauce in saucepan. Cook and stir 1 minute or until thickened. Add celery and pineapple; cook 2 minutes longer. Serve over cod with rice. Makes 4 servings.

135 calories per serving
3.6 grams fat per serving
325 mg sodium per serving
45 mg cholesterol per serving

The lingcod is neither a ling or a cod, but a member of the greenling family. Lingcod vary in weight from 5-20 pounds. They range from the Baja Peninsula of Mexico to Northwest Alaska, but are most abundant in the colder waters of the north. The fillets are white, medium firm in texture and have a delicious flavor.

← SALMON PIQUANTE →

1 medium onion, thinly sliced
1 lemon, thinly sliced
1 clove garlic, minced
1 teaspoon mixed pickling spice
¼ teaspoon salt
1½ lbs. salmon fillets or steaks
¼ cup mayonnaise
¼ cup plain low fat yogurt
¼ cucumber, finely chopped and peeled

Spread onion, lemon, garlic and spices on bottom of baking dish. Arrange salmon on top, thickest portions toward outside of dish. Cover tightly with plastic wrap. Microwave 5 minutes on HIGH. Mix mayonnaise, plain low fat yogurt and cucumber and spread over salmon. Microwave on HIGH until fish flakes. Garnish with lemon twists and parsley sprigs. Makes 6 servings.

240 calories per serving
15 grams fat per serving
200 mg sodium per serving
70 mg cholesterol per serving

◆── SALMON STEAKS ──◆
LIMONE

1 tablespoon "Barbecue Basting Sauce"
1 teaspoon lemon juice
1 lb. salmon steaks or fillets

Combine Barbecue Basting Sauce and lemon juice in microwave container and melt. Arrange salmon steaks in baking dish with meatiest portions to outside of dish. Brush with sauce. Cover with plastic wrap. Microwave according to manufacturer's directions or about 3 minutes per pound. Makes 4 servings.

190 calories per serving
11 grams fat per serving
90 mg sodium per serving
70 mg cholesterol per serving

MICROWAVE BAKED TROUT

1 trout, about 6 oz.
½ tablespoon polyunsaturated margarine
1 slice onion
1 slice lemon
pepper to taste

Gut trout; remove head and tail, and fillet if desired. Place margarine, onion, lemon and pepper in inner cavity and secure with a toothpick. Place trout in baking dish with backbone facing outward and cover with plastic wrap. Microwave on HIGH for 2½-3½ minutes. Makes 1 serving.

For 2 trout microwave 5-7 minutes.
3 trout microwave 7½-10 minutes.
4 trout microwave 10-14 minutes.

245 calories per serving
16.9 grams fat per serving
122 mg sodium per serving
50 mg cholesterol per serving

If there is a lingering odor in your microwave after cooking seafood, boil a half of a fresh lemon for 5 minutes. The fresh lemon aroma will freshen up the microwave.

MICROWAVE STEAMED CLAMS

"A Meal In A Hurry"

24 large or 45 small clams in shells
½ cup water

Wash shellfish thoroughly, discarding any broken or open shells. Set aside. Pour water in 2 quart casserole; cover. Microwave at HIGH until water boils. Add shellfish; cover dish. Microwave at HIGH until shellfish open, 3-4 minutes, stirring about half the cooking time. Serve with "Barbecue Basting Sauce" (page 201), hot french bread, cucumber slices and pineapple chunks. Makes 4 servings.

oysters or mussels in the shell may be substituted for clams

90 calories per serving
2 grams fat per serving
90 mg sodium per serving
40 mg cholesterol per serving

◆── LOBSTER TAILS ──◆

1 lb. lobster tails (7 to 8 ozs. each) or
1 lb. slipper lobster tails, defrosted
1 tablespoon polyunsaturated margarine, melted
1 clove garlic, minced

Split each lobster tail through top shell and release meat, leaving it connected to shell at one end. Pull meat through slit and place on top of shell. Arrange tails in baking dish and brush with margarine melted, with garlic added. Cover with plastic wrap. Microwave 3 minutes on HIGH or until meat is opaque and shell turns red. Overcooking causes meat to toughen. Makes 2 servings.

150 calories per serving
9 grams fat per serving
280 mg sodium per serving
90 mg cholesterol per serving

All of the lobster is edible except for the bony shell structure, the small crop or craw in the head of the lobster, and the dark vein running down the back of the body meat. The green material is the liver or tomalley. This is excellent eating, as is the red or coral, which is the lobster's underdeveloped spawn.

A fresh lobster varies from shades of green, brown or occasionally deep blue. The bright red color of the lobster is obtained only by cooking.

Cook a lobster by dropping it head first into a pot of lightly salted boiling water. When the water starts to boil again, allow ten minutes for a 1 pound lobster and two or three minutes for each additional pound.

Have a beach party by using seawater to cook the lobster. This gives an excellent flavor to the meat.

MICROWAVE SHRIMP OR PRAWNS

2 tablespoons polyunsaturated margarine
2 tablespoons dried parsley flakes
2 tablespoons lemon juice
1 clove garlic, minced
¼ cup white wine
1 lb. raw jumbo shrimp or prawns, peeled and deveined
paprika

Place margarine in 2-quart casserole. Microwave at HIGH until melted, about 30 seconds. Stir in parsley, lemon juice, garlic and wine. Add seafood; toss to coat. Cover dish. Microwave at HIGH until seafood is pink, opaque and tender, 1-2 minutes. Sprinkle with paprika. Serve with fruit compote and rice. Makes 4 servings.

165 calories per serving
6.5 grams fat per serving
230 mg sodium per serving
180 mg cholesterol per serving

STUFFED JUMBO SHRIMP (SCAMPI)

2 lbs. large shrimp or scampi, in the shell
1 tablespoon polyunsaturated margarine
¼ cup celery, finely chopped
1 small onion, finely chopped
1 tablespoon polyunsaturated margarine, melted
½ cup bread crumbs
¼ teaspoon basil
½ teaspoon parsley, chopped
¼ teaspoon garlic salt

Peel shrimp, leaving shell on tail section. Lay on back. With a sharp knife, split almost through (butterfly cut). Devein. Combine celery, onion and margarine in a 1-quart casserole. Microwave 3 minutes on HIGH, or until onion is transparent. Stir in remaining ingredients. Brush shrimp with melted margarine. Spoon 1 tablespoon of mixture into butterflied area of shrimp. Place in baking dish with tail resting straight up on the side of dish. Microwave 3 minutes on HIGH or until shrimp are opaque. Do not overcook. Time varies slightly with size of shrimp. Makes 4 servings.

200 calories per serving
8 grams fat per serving
425 mg sodium per serving
160 mg cholesterol per serving

SPECIALTIES

GRILLED SHARK TERIYAKI

1½ lbs. shark steaks, or other firm-fleshed fish
(swordfish, orange roughy or albacore tuna)
1 - 20 oz. can pineapple chunks, drained
(reserve juice for marinade)

◆

Marinade:
3 tablespoons pineapple juice
3 tablespoons light soy sauce
2 tablespoons sherry
1 tablespoon fresh ginger, grated
½ teaspoon dry mustard
2 cloves garlic, minced
1 teaspoon brown sugar

◆

1-2 large green peppers, cubed

Place shark in a covered 2-quart bowl. Set aside. Drain pineapple, reserving 3 tablespoons of juice; set pineapple chunks aside. To make marinade: in a bowl combine reserved juice, soy sauce, sherry, ginger, mustard, garlic and brown sugar. Stir well. Pour over shark, cover and marinate in refrigerator for one hour, turning once. Using bamboo or metal skewers, make kabobs by alternating pineapple and green pepper. Drain shark, reserving marinade. Place on lightly-oiled grate 4-5 inches from hot briquettes and cook 4-5 minutes (or broil in oven). Baste with marinade and turn. Cook an additional 4-5 minutes or until shark flakes when tested with a fork. Baste fruit and vegetable kabobs and place on grill. Cook 15-30 seconds on each side, or until just browned. Serve with raw carrots and celery and french roll. Makes 4 servings.

250 calories per serving
1.5 grams fat per serving
625 mg sodium per serving

◆── SAN FRANCISCO ──▶ STYLE SHARK

2 tablespoons polyunsaturated oil
1 cup mushrooms, sliced
¼ cup onion, chopped
1 clove garlic, minced
1 - 16 oz. can tomatoes, broken up
1 tablespoon parsley, minced
½ teaspoon oregano, crushed
dash pepper
1 lb. shark fillets

Heat oil in frypan or skillet; add mushrooms, onion and garlic and sauté. Add remaining ingredients, except shark and bring to a boil. Simmer uncovered, 10 minutes, stirring occasionally. Cut shark into serving-sized pieces and add to tomato mixture. Cover and cook over medium heat 8-10 minutes or until shark flakes when tested with a fork. Serve with rice. Makes 4 servings.

220 calories per serving
8 grams fat per serving
670 mg sodium per serving

PORTUGUESE SKATE WINGS

2 tablespoons polyunsaturated margarine, melted
1 cup mushrooms, sliced
1 medium onion, sliced
2 tablespoons flour
½ cup white wine
1 - 20 oz. can tomatoes, undrained
½ teaspoon pepper
¼ teaspoon oregano
¼ teaspoon thyme
1½ lbs. skate wings

Melt margarine in large skillet. Sauté mushrooms and onions over moderate heat until lightly and evenly browned. Sprinkle flour over mixture in skillet and stir to make smooth paste. Slowly stir in wine. Add tomatoes and seasonings and cook over low heat, stirring constantly, until thickened. Place skate wings in tomato mixture in skillet. Cover and simmer for 15 minutes or until fish flakes when tested with a fork. Serve with pasta. Makes 6 servings.

315 calories per serving
7.5 grams fat per serving

Skate wings have a delicate and distinctive flavor, much like that of scallops. It is an ideal fish for children and the elderly, because it is boneless and easily digested.

STIR-FRY SWORDFISH AND VEGETABLES

1 lb. swordfish, steaks or fillets
pepper to taste
1 tablespoon polyunsaturated oil
2 carrots, diagonally cut in thin slices
1 medium onion, thinly sliced
3 zucchini, cut in ¼-inch slices
¼ teaspoon thyme leaves, crushed

Cut swordfish into 1½-inch chunks; sprinkle with pepper and set aside. In hot oil, stir-fry vegetables with thyme until vegetables are tender-crisp. Add fish and stir-fry until fish flakes when tested with a fork. Serve with brown rice. Makes 4 servings.

200 calories per serving
10.8 grams fat per serving
950 mg sodium per serving
55 mg cholesterol per serving

Swordfish, also known as billfish, are found in temperate and tropical seas throughout the world. The average weight is 200-400 pounds, but they may reach 1,000 pounds and 15 feet in length. This high-protein fish has a distinctive flavor and firm flesh. Swordfish steaks can be broiled, baked, poached and barbecued. The swordfish catch does not always meet the demand, so this fish will remain a high-priced item.

◆— SWORDFISH WITH GARLIC —◆

"A Twenty Minute Meal"

Seasoned margarine:
1 tablespoon polyunsaturated margarine
4 cloves garlic, minced
pepper to taste
2 tablespoons vermouth

◆

2 lbs. swordfish steaks

To make seasoned margarine: melt margarine in saucepan. Add garlic and sauté until garlic begins to color. Season with pepper and add vermouth. Place fish on broiler pan and baste with seasoned margarine. Broil 4 inches from heat for 10-15 minutes or until fish flakes when tested with a fork. Baste occasionally with seasoned margarine. Makes 8 servings.

160 calories per serving
6.5 grams fat per serving
95 mg sodium per serving
55 mg cholesterol per serving

LANGOSTINO SAUTÉ WITH ALMONDS AND GRAPES

½ lb. langostinos or prawns, cooked and shelled
2 teaspoons polyunsaturated margarine
¼ cup onion, finely chopped
1 teaspoon brown sugar
1 teaspoon Dijon mustard
2 tablespoons white wine
½ cup fresh grapes, seedless
2 tablespoons almonds, dry roasted, chopped
lemon wedges
parsley, chopped

Sauté langostinos or prawns with onions in margarine about 4 minutes. Add brown sugar, mustard, wine and grapes. Toss until onions are tender-crisp, grapes are heated through and all ingredients are nicely coated with pan sauce. Do not overcook. Serve sprinkled with toasted almonds; garnish with lemon wedges and parsley. Serve immediately. Makes 2 servings.

225 calories per serving
9.5 grams fat per serving
250 mg sodium per serving
90 mg cholesterol per serving

Langostino is from South America and part of the lobster family.

MARINATED ORIENTAL OCTOPUS

"Great For A Party"

5 lbs. octopus legs
2 quarts water
2 bay leaves
¼ teaspoon salt
1 tablespoon Chinese vinegar
1 cup vinegar
¼ cup sugar
¼ cup polyunsaturated oil
½ cup white wine
2 tablespoons light soy sauce
2 tablespoons lemon juice
¼ cup green onion, sliced
1 teaspoon garlic powder
sesame seeds
Japanese horseradish

Prepare octopus by boiling legs in water, bay leaves, salt and Chinese vinegar for ½ hour. Cool. Skin, if desired. Slice into thin rounds. Combine vinegar, sugar, oil, wine, light soy sauce, lemon juice, onion and garlic powder. Let stand several hours or overnight to blend flavors. To serve, drain sliced octopus and place on a platter with a bowl of marinade sauce, sesame seeds and Japanese horseradish. Dip octopus into sauce, then seeds and horseradish. Makes 30-3 oz. servings.

75 calories per serving
4.8 grams fat per serving
85 mg cholesterol per serving

MARINATED CALAMARI (SQUID) SALAD

1 lb. cleaned squid mantles (bodies)
1 tablespoon olive oil
1 teaspoon Dijon mustard
3 cloves garlic, minced
dash red pepper (cayenne)
1 tablespoon lemon juice
⅛ teaspoon dried basil
½ teaspoon pepper
¼ red onion, thinly sliced
1 green pepper, cut into chunks
1 tablespoon parsley, chopped
2 large tomatoes, chunked

Cut squid mantles (bodies) into rounds or rings. In medium skillet combine oil, mustard, garlic, red pepper, lemon juice, basil and pepper. Bring to boil and add squid. Sauté for 30 seconds or until squid turns white; remove from heat. Transfer to bowl. Stir in onion and green pepper and cover. Refrigerate 2-4 hours or overnight. Before serving, toss in parsley and tomatoes. Makes 4 servings.

160 calories per serving
4.7 grams fat per serving
195 mg sodium per serving

Squid (calamari) is a free swimming mollusk. Squid range in size from 1 inch to 60 feet. The most common size found in the market is under 10 inches. Most squid in the market has been frozen. Freezing preserves quality and provides protection during handling. The flesh is firm and delicately flavored. It is very popular in Mediterranean and Oriental ethnic groups.

STIR FRIED SQUID (CALAMARI)

1¼ lbs. whole squid or 1 lb. cleaned squid

♦

Marinade:
2 tablespoons light soy sauce
⅛ teaspoon pepper
2 tablespoons white wine
2 teaspoons cornstarch
1 tablespoon sesame oil

♦

1 tablespoon polyunsaturated oil
1 teaspoon fresh ginger, grated
2 cloves garlic, minced
½ cup mushrooms, sliced
½ medium red or green pepper, cut into thin strips
¼ cup green onion, sliced
½ cup peas, frozen

Clean squid. Cut mantles (bodies) widthwise into ¼-inch strips; chop tentacles. To make marinade: Combine soy sauce, pepper, wine, cornstarch and sesame oil; mix well. Add squid; marinate at room temperature while preparing remaining ingredients. In large skillet or wok, heat oil. Add ginger and garlic; stir fry for 30 seconds. Add squid and vegetables with marinade; stir-fry briefly until squid is just cooked through, approximately 45 seconds. Serve immediately over hot rice. Makes 4 servings.

200 calories per serving
8 grams fat per serving
550 mg sodium per serving

STUFFED CALAMARI (SQUID)

1¼ lbs. whole squid or 1 lb. cleaned squid

Stuffing:
¾ cup part-skim mozzarella cheese, grated
2 tablespoons parsley, chopped
1 teaspoon dried oregano
1 teaspoon dried basil
⅓ cup Parmesan cheese
½ cup bread crumbs
⅓ cup onions, finely chopped
1 cup mushrooms, chopped

2 cups marinara sauce (see page 169)
2 tablespoons Parmesan cheese, grated
¼ cup part-skim mozzarella cheese, grated for topping

Clean squid, keeping mantles (bodies) whole. To make stuffing: Combine cheese, parsley, oregano, basil and Parmesan cheese; mix well. Stir in bread crumbs, onions and mushrooms. Stuff squid until plump, but not packed. Close opening and secure with toothpick. Pour small amount of marinara sauce into 11x7 inch glass or ceramic baking dish. Arrange squid in single layer in baking dish. Top with marinara sauce and 2 tablespoons Parmesan cheese. Bake uncovered at 350° for 20 minutes. Top with mozzarella cheese and bake an additional 10 minutes or until squid is tender. Makes 4 servings.

MARINARA SAUCE

1 tablespoon olive oil
4 cloves garlic, chopped
1 cup onion, chopped
1 cup mushrooms, chopped
1 - 28 oz. can whole tomatoes, undrained
½ teaspoon dried oregano
½ teaspoon dried basil
¼ teaspoon pepper
½ teaspoon sugar

In large skillet, heat olive oil. Add garlic, onion, and mushrooms and sauté until just tender. Stir in remaining ingredients, breaking up tomatoes with spoon. Cook over medium heat until sauce thickens, approximately 30 minutes. Serve over hot pasta. Makes about 3 cups sauce.

Stuffed calamari with sauce:
350 calories per serving
9 grams fat per serving
740 mg sodium per serving

INTERNATIONAL

◆— ORIENTAL STIR- —◆ FRY WITH ALBACORE (TUNA)

Charlie is out of the can!

1 lb. fresh/frozen albacore (tuna)

◆

Marinade:
½ cup white wine
1 teaspoon ground or fresh ginger
1 teaspoon garlic powder or 2 cloves garlic, minced
½ teaspoon onion powder
½ teaspoon pepper
2 teaspoons sugar
1 tablespoon sesame oil

◆

1 tablespoon polyunsaturated margarine
2 cups mushrooms, sliced
½ cup celery, sliced on the diagonal
½ cup green onion, chopped
1 cup broccoli, sliced on the diagonal

Cut fish into 1-inch chunks. To make marinade: Combine wine, ginger, garlic, onion powder, pepper, sugar and sesame oil. Marinate fish for 15 minutes. Melt margarine in a wok or frying pan. Add vegetables and cook until tender-crisp. Add fish with marinade to vegetables and cook at medium heat until fish flakes. Serve with brown rice and fresh fruit plate. Makes 4 servings.

200 calories per serving
8 grams fat per serving
145 mg sodium per serving
50 mg cholesterol per serving

Don't be turned off when you first see albacore tuna. The meat will be somewhat pinkish colored and a little soft. We promise you white firm fillets when it is cooked.

◆ ITALIAN FLOUNDER ◆ ROLLUPS

1 lb. flounder or cod fillets, skinless
1 - 10 oz. package frozen french-style green beans
2 tablespoons onion, chopped
1 - 8 oz. can tomato sauce
¼ teaspoon oregano leaves
¼ teaspoon basil leaves
⅛ teaspoon garlic powder
2 tablespoons Parmesan cheese, grated

Divide fish into 4 servings. Set aside. Add green beans and onion to ¼ cup boiling water. Cover and boil gently until beans are tender-crisp, about 7 minutes. Drain. Place ¼ of the green bean-onion mixture in middle of each fish portion. Start with narrow end of fillet and roll. Place in baking pan, with the end of fillets underneath. Mix tomato sauce, oregano, basil and garlic powder. Pour over fish rollups. Sprinkle with cheese. Bake at 400° until fish flakes when tested with a fork, about 15-20 minutes. Serve with yellow summer squash and bran muffins. Makes 4 servings.

125 calories per serving
1.5 grams fat per serving
400 mg sodium per serving
50 mg cholesterol per serving

◆ ORIENTAL HALIBUT ◆ SAUTÉ

1 clove garlic, minced
2 tablespoons polyunsaturated margarine
2 cups mushrooms, sliced
1 lb. halibut, skinless, cut into 1-inch cubes
½ cup white wine
2 tablespoons light soy sauce
¼ cup green onion, sliced

Sauté garlic in melted margarine. Add mushrooms; sauté and stir 1 minute. Add halibut to mushroom mixture and sauté 2-3 minutes. Add wine and soy sauce and bring to a boil. Reduce heat and simmer until fish flakes when tested with a fork. Sprinkle with green onions and serve over rice. Makes 4 servings.

215 calories per serving
6.9 grams fat per serving
545 mg sodium per serving
55 mg cholesterol per serving

GRILLED HALIBUT MEXICANA WITH SALSA

1 lb. halibut steaks or fillets

◆

Marinade:
⅓ cup lime juice
3 cloves garlic, minced
1 tablespoon polyunsaturated oil
¼ cup beer
1 tablespoon parsley, chopped
½ teaspoon cumin
2 teaspoons Dijon mustard
pepper to taste

◆

Salsa

Place halibut in marinade dish and set aside. Combine remaining ingredients except Salsa; pour over halibut. Cover and marinate in refrigerator for 1 hour, turning once. While halibut is marinating, make Salsa. Drain halibut reserving marinade. Place on lightly-oiled grill, 4-5 inches from hot coals. Cook 4-5 minutes; baste with marinade and turn. Cook an additional 4-5 minutes, or until halibut flakes when tested with a fork. Top with Salsa. Makes 4 servings.

SALSA

2 medium tomatoes, peeled, seeded and coarsely chopped
¼ cup red onion, chopped
3 tablespoons green chiles, diced
2-3 dashes liquid hot pepper sauce

Combine all ingredients and blend well. Let stand at room temperature or in refrigerator for 15-20 minutes to blend flavors. Makes about 1¼ cups sauce.

190 calories per serving
5 grams fat per serving
100 mg sodium per serving
55 mg cholesterol per serving

MACADAMIA BAKED MAHI MAHI

6 tablespoons flour
¼ teaspoon onion powder
⅛ teaspoon pepper
1 tablespoon polyunsaturated margarine
1 lb. mahi mahi
6 macadamia nuts, chopped

Combine flour and seasonings. Melt margarine in shallow baking dish in oven. Dredge mahi mahi in flour mixture; place in dish. Turn mahi mahi to coat with margarine; place in baking dish and sprinkle with macadamia nuts. Bake at 400° for 10 minutes or until mahi mahi flakes when tested with a fork. Serve with fresh pineapple slices and sweet potatoes. Makes 4 servings.

215 calories per serving
8.0 grams fat per serving
155 mg sodium per serving
90 mg cholesterol per serving

Mahi-Mahi is the popular Hawaiian name for the dolphinfish, which is not related to the marine mammal called the dolphin. Found in tropical and subtropical waters throughout the world, dolphinfish inhabit the warmer waters of both the Atlantic and Pacific coasts. The white flesh is firm, with solid flakes and delicate flavor. Mahi-Mahi is considered by many to be one of the most delicious seafoods.

MONKFISH WITH ORIENTAL SAUCE

"A Family Favorite"

Sauce:
¼ cup orange juice
2 tablespoons polyunsaturated oil
2 tablespoons light soy sauce
1 tablespoon lemon juice
1 clove garlic, minced
⅛ teaspoon pepper

*2 lbs. monkfish fillets or steaks, or
other white-fleshed fish*

Combine sauce ingredients. Brush all sides of fish with sauce. Place fish on lightly-oiled grill or barbecue over hot coals or broil in oven. Brush fish frequently with sauce during cooking. Serve with baked potatoes and steamed carrots. Makes 8 servings.

120 calories per serving
4.7 grams fat per serving
40 mg cholesterol per serving

◆ SEAFOOD ROLLUPS ◆ IN ITALIAN SAUCE (POLLOCK)

Italian sauce:
2 small onions, chopped
1 clove garlic, minced
2 tablespoons polyunsaturated oil
1 - 3¹⁄₃ oz. can mushrooms, sliced
1 - 8 oz. can tomato sauce and 1 can water
¹⁄₄ cup parsley, chopped
3 tablespoons lemon juice
¹⁄₄ cup white wine
¹⁄₄ teaspoon rosemary, dried
1 teaspoon sugar

◆

2 lbs. pollock fillets or other white-fleshed fish fillets
¹⁄₂ cup Parmesan cheese

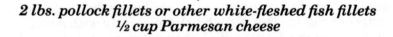

To make Italian sauce: Sauté onions and garlic in hot oil until onions are transparent. Add mushrooms, tomato sauce, water, parsley, lemon juice, wine and seasonings; simmer about 30 minutes. Place 2 tablespoons of sauce in the middle of each fillet. Roll up like jelly rolls. Place in a shallow baking dish, with the ends underneath, to keep them from unrolling. Pour remaining sauce over the fish rolls. Sprinkle with Parmesan cheese. Bake at 400° for 20 minutes or until fish flakes when tested with a fork. Serve with pasta and vegetables. Makes 8 servings.

180 calories per serving
6 grams fat per serving
360 mg sodium per serving
75 mg cholesterol per serving

◆─ GINGER STEAMED ─◆ WHOLE ROCKFISH (SNAPPER)

1 dressed fish (about 3 lbs.)
(mackerel, salmon or rockfish)
1 tablespoon polyunsaturated margarine
lemon juice
1 medium onion, thinly sliced
lemon, thinly sliced
pepper
fresh grated ginger

Rinse fish. In fish cavity, insert bits of margarine, lemon juice, onion and lemon slices. Sprinkle inside and outside with pepper and ginger. Wrap loosely in foil. Place fish on rack directly over boiling water in large pot. Cover and simmer about 6-10 minutes per pound. Do not overcook. Makes 6 servings.

Invite friends over for a Chinese dinner. Serve Ginger Steamed Fish with favorite Chinese dishes.

200 calories per serving
10 grams fat per serving
95 mg sodium per serving
75 mg cholesterol per serving

MEXICAN STYLE LIME ROCKFISH (SNAPPER)

¼ cup green onion, chopped
1 tablespoon polyunsaturated margarine
2 medium tomatoes, chopped
3 tablespoons fresh lime juice
1 oz. canned green chiles, diced
1 tablespoon parsley, minced
⅛ teaspoon salt
⅛ teaspoon garlic powder
pepper to taste
1 lb. rockfish, snapper or other white-fleshed fish fillets
lime wedges

Sauté onion in margarine until tender. Add remaining ingredients except fish and lime wedges. Bring to a boil; reduce heat and simmer 10 minutes. Place snapper in skillet; spoon sauce over fish. Cover and simmer 10 minutes, or until fish flakes when tested with a fork. Serve with Spanish rice and papaya. Garnish with lime wedges. Makes 4 servings.

130 calories per serving
4.4 grams fat per serving
185 mg sodium per serving
60 mg cholesterol per serving

TERIYAKI SABLEFISH (BLACK COD)

Marinade:
1 tablespoon light soy sauce
2 tablespoons sherry
1 clove garlic, minced
½ teaspoon fresh ginger root or ¼ teaspoon ground ginger
1 teaspoon honey

◆

½ lb. sablefish (black cod) steaks
lemon wedges

To make marinade: Combine soy sauce, sherry, garlic, ginger and honey. Marinate sablefish in soy mixture about 1 hour; turn after 30 minutes. Broil 4 inches from heat about 10-15 minutes or until fish flakes when tested with a fork. Garnish with lemon wedges. Serve with rice. Makes 2 servings.

165 calories per serving
5.6 grams fat per serving
450 mg sodium per serving
65 mg cholesterol per serving

SCANDINAVIAN SALMON STEAKS WITH SPINACH

1 lb. salmon steaks
pepper
1 teaspoon dill weed
1 tablespoon polyunsaturated margarine
1 large onion, chopped
1 clove garlic, finely minced
2 lbs. fresh spinach, washed, with leaves cut into 1-inch
wide strips
lemon slices

Arrange salmon on a lightly-oiled broiler pan; broil 4 inches from the heat for 5 minutes. Turn steaks and season with pepper. Sprinkle with dill weed. Broil steaks for about 5 minutes more or until fish flakes when tested with a fork. Meanwhile, in a large frying pan, melt margarine and sauté the onion and garlic until tender. Stir in the spinach (with the water that clings to the leaves). Cover pan and cook over high heat for about 3 minutes. Stir occasionally. To serve, spoon spinach onto a rimmed serving platter. Lay salmon steaks and lemon on top. Serve with boiled new potatoes. Makes 4 servings.

225 calories per serving
11 grams fat per serving
250 mg sodium per serving
75 mg cholesterol per serving

◆──── SALMON PLAKI ────◆

2 lbs. salmon fillets
pepper to taste
1 teaspoon dried oregano
2 cloves garlic, minced
2 tablespoons polyunsaturated oil or olive oil
1 tomato, thinly sliced
1 onion, thinly sliced
½ cup parsley, minced
1 lemon, thinly sliced
½ cup dry bread crumbs

Place fish in lightly-oiled baking pan and sprinkle with pepper, oregano, garlic and oil. Layer with tomato slices, onion rings and parsley. Top with lemon slices and bread crumbs. Bake at 375° for 30 minutes. NOTE: You may wish to cover the dish loosely with foil half-way through baking to prevent lemons from becoming too crisp. Serve with whole grain rolls, steamed rice and fresh fruit. Makes 8 servings.

225 calories per serving
12 grams fat per serving
10 mg sodium per serving
55 mg cholesterol per serving

Plaki is a Greek word for baked fish.

← SALMON TERIYAKI →

Marinade:
3 tablespoons light soy sauce
¼ cup white wine
½ cup brown sugar
½ teaspoon ground ginger or
1 teaspoon fresh ginger, grated

1 lb. salmon steaks or fillets

To make marinade: combine soy sauce, wine, brown sugar and ginger in a bowl. Add salmon and marinate for ½ hour. Drain salmon. Broil or barbecue fish about 4 inches from heat source. Cook until fish flakes when tested with a fork. Serve with rice and steamed brussel sprouts. Makes 4 servings.

225 calories per serving
7.7 grams fat per serving
450 mg sodium per serving
75 mg cholesterol per serving

Teriyaki marinade can be reused for up to two weeks, if it is refrigerated in airtight containers.

FETTUCCINE WITH SALMON

2 tablespoons polyunsaturated margarine
1½ cups mushrooms, sliced
2 tablespoons onions, chopped
1 small yellow squash or zucchini, sliced
1 tablespoon flour
⅛ teaspoon basil
⅛ teaspoon oregano, crushed
½ cup skim milk
¾ cup salmon, cooked and flaked, or canned
½ cup frozen peas, thawed
½ cup tomato, diced
1 tablespoon parsley, minced
1 tablespoon white wine
8 oz. fettuccine, cooked and drained
pepper to taste
lemon wedges

Melt margarine in skillet. Add mushrooms, onion and squash and sauté until tender-crisp. Add flour and herbs; cook and stir 1 minute. Slowly add skim milk, stirring and cooking over medium heat until thickened. Add salmon, peas, tomato, parsley and wine. Heat thoroughly. Toss hot fettuccine with vegetable mixture. Season with pepper. Place on warm platter. Garnish with lemon wedges. Makes 6 servings.

Excellent use for leftover poached or barbecued salmon.

270 calories per serving
8 grams fat per serving
110 mg sodium per serving
40 mg cholesterol per serving

HOT CURRY SALMON-RICE PILAF

1 - 15½ oz. can salmon
2 cups cooked rice
1 cup celery, thinly sliced
½ cup parsley, chopped
¼ cup mayonnaise
¼ cup low fat yogurt
2 tablespoons lemon juice
1 tablespoon curry powder
paprika

Drain and break salmon into large pieces. Combine rice, celery, parsley and salmon in a medium bowl. Combine mayonnaise, yogurt, lemon juice and curry powder. Add mayonnaise mixture to salmon mixture; toss lightly. Place in 6 lightly-oiled, 6 oz. casseroles or custard cups. Sprinkle with paprika. Bake in a 400° oven for 15-20 minutes or until heated. Serve hot with pear salad and whole wheat roll. Makes 8 servings.

A great idea for a potluck dinner.

190 calories per serving
10 grams fat per serving
345 mg sodium per serving
30 mg cholesterol per serving

◆—MEDITERRANEAN—◆ STYLE SEA BASS

2 lbs. sea bass, rockfish (snapper), sole or halibut fillets
3 tablespoons polyunsaturated margarine, melted
pepper
2 cloves garlic, minced
½ cup green onion, finely chopped
½ cup celery, finely chopped
¼ cup green pepper, finely chopped
½ teaspoon oregano
1 tablespoon sugar
¼ teaspoon pepper
1 - 8 oz. can tomato sauce
½ cup white wine
⅓ cup bread crumbs
⅓ cup Parmesan cheese

Cut fish into 8 portions. Pour melted margarine in 9x13 inch pan. Place fillets in pan and sprinkle with pepper. In bowl combine garlic, onions, celery, green pepper, oregano, sugar and pepper with tomato sauce and wine. Pour on top of fillets. Sprinkle bread crumbs and cheese over top of fillets. Bake uncovered in 400° oven for 20-30 minutes or until fish flakes when tested with a fork and top is browned. Serve with hot rice, green salad and hot garlic bread. Makes 8 servings.

195 calories per serving
6 grams fat per serving
400 mg sodium per serving
70 mg cholesterol per serving

◆ SOLE FLORENTINE ◆
"Excellent for Entertaining"

Stuffing:
1 tablespoon polyunsaturated margarine
½ cup mushrooms, sliced
1 - 10 oz. package frozen spinach
⅓ cup green onion, sliced
1 cup cooked rice
½ teaspoon dill weed
¼ teaspoon pepper

1½ lbs. sole

Sauce:
1 tablespoon polyunsaturated margarine
2 tablespoons flour
1¼ cups skim milk
¾ cup part-skim mozzarella cheese, grated
1 teaspoon Worcestershire sauce
½ teaspoon dry mustard
dash red pepper (cayenne)

lemon slices
parsley

To prepare stuffing: Melt 1 tablespoon margarine in skillet; add mushrooms, spinach and green onion; cook until tender. Add rice, dill weed and pepper. Lay out sole fillets; divide stuffing among fillets. Roll up and fasten with toothpicks. Place in a lightly-oiled shallow baking dish. Bake in a 400° oven for 15-20 minutes or until fish flakes. To prepare sauce: In a saucepan, melt 1 tablespoon margarine. Add flour and cook, stirring until bubbly and smooth. Remove from heat and gradually blend in milk. Add remaining ingredients. Cook over moderate heat, stirring until thickened and smooth. Serve over fish. Garnish with lemon slices and parsley. Makes 6 servings.

295 calories per serving
8.7 grams fat per serving
410 mg sodium per serving
65 mg cholesterol per serving

BEAN SPROUT TUNA CHOW MEIN

"Stretch A Can Of Tuna"

1 chicken bouillon cube
1 cup boiling water
1 tablespoon light soy sauce
pepper to taste
1 tablespoon cornstarch
1 tablespoon cold water
2 tablespoons polyunsaturated oil
6 stalks celery, cut diagonally
2 medium onions, chopped
1 - 6 oz. can bamboo shoots, drained
1 green pepper, chopped
½ cup mushrooms, sliced
2 cups bean sprouts
1 - 7 oz. can tuna, drained

Dissolve bouillon cube in boiling water; add soy sauce and pepper. Mix cornstarch in cold water until dissolved. Add slowly to bouillon mixture. Set aside. Heat oil in frying pan or wok over high heat. When hot, toss in celery and onion; stir-fry 3 minutes. Add bamboo shoots, green pepper, mushrooms and bean sprouts. Continue to stir-fry 2-3 minutes longer. Stir broth mixture into vegetables. Stir and cook just until sauce is thickened. Add tuna and stir until hot and sauce is clear. Serve immediately over rice. Makes 4 servings.

215 calories per serving
7.5 grams fat per serving
600 mg sodium per serving
30 mg cholesterol per serving

PASTA WITH MUSSEL OR CLAM SAUCE

6 ripe tomatoes, medium size
2 tablespoons parsley, chopped
1 teaspoon dried basil, crumbled
2 tablespoons lemon juice
1 clove garlic, minced
¼ teaspoon pepper
1 lb. mussels or clams, ground
1 lb. linguini or other pasta
Parmesan cheese, grated

Dip tomatoes in boiling water until skin comes off easily, about 30 seconds. Peel and chop. Combine with parsley, basil, lemon juice, garlic, pepper and shellfish in a saucepan. Bring to boil. Reduce heat and simmer, uncovered, for 15-20 minutes. Stir occasionally. Cook pasta in boiling water following package directions and drain. Return to kettle and toss with about ⅓ of the sauce. Divide among 6 deep plates. Top with remaining sauce and serve at once. Sprinkle with Parmesan cheese, if desired. Serve with green salad and french bread. Makes 6 servings.

Sauce:
90 calories per serving
2.9 grams fat per serving
65 mg sodium per serving
30 mg cholesterol per serving

← PARADISE PRAWN → SAUTÉ

"A Light Meal For Two"

¼ cup unsweetened pineapple juice (drained from can)
1 tablespoon light soy sauce
⅛ teaspoon ground ginger
1 tablespoon cold water
1 teaspoon cornstarch
½ lb. shrimp or prawns, fresh or frozen,
peeled and deveined
½ cup unsweetened pineapple chunks, drained
½ cup peas, fresh or frozen
1 stalk celery, diagonally sliced
1 green onion, slivered

Combine in saucepan pineapple juice, soy sauce, ginger, cold water and cornstarch; bring to boil. Reduce heat and stir until thick and clear. Add shrimp, pineapple, peas, celery and green onion and sauté for 5 minutes, or until thoroughly heated and shrimp are heated; stir frequently. Serve over rice. Makes 2 servings.

200 calories per serving
1.5 grams fat per serving
635 mg sodium per serving
160 mg cholesterol per serving

SAUCES
DRESSINGS AND DIPS

ZESTY
COCKTAIL SAUCE

"Excellent for shrimp cocktail"

1 - 8 oz. can tomato sauce
2 tablespoons chili sauce
¼ teaspoon garlic powder
dash oregano
¼ teaspoon liquid hot pepper sauce
¼ teaspoon thyme
⅛ teaspoon sugar
dash basil

Combine all ingredients in a small saucepan. Simmer 10-12 minutes, stirring occasionally. Serve hot or cold. Excellent as a cocktail sauce on shrimp or crab appetizer. Use as a sauce for poached white-fleshed fish. Makes about 1 cup sauce.

8 calories per tablespoon
0 grams fat per tablespoon
110 mg sodium per tablespoon
0 grams cholesterol per tablespoon

SKINNY-DIP TARTAR SAUCE

¾ cup low fat cottage cheese
¼ cup low fat yogurt
1 tablespoon onion, chopped
2 tablespoons cucumber, grated
1 tablespoon fresh parsley, minced
1 teaspoon celery flakes

Blend cottage cheese in blender until smooth. Mix all other ingredients and refrigerate. Makes 1 cup.

12 calories per tablespoon
.2 grams fat per tablespoon
25 mg sodium per tablespoon
1 mg cholesterol per tablespoon

◆— HEART HEALTHY —➤ TARTAR SAUCE OR DIP

8 oz. plain low fat yogurt
½ cup cucumber, diced
½ cup celery, diced
½ cup carrot, shredded
1 tablespoon onion, finely chopped
½ teaspoon paprika
1 tablespoon Worcestershire sauce
1 teaspoon lemon juice

In a medium bowl combine yogurt, cucumber, celery, carrot, onion, paprika, Worcestershire sauce and lemon juice; mix well. Cover and chill for one hour. Use as a tartar sauce for seafood or as a dip for raw vegetables such as mushrooms, celery, or carrot sticks. Makes 1¾ cups or 28-1 tablespoon servings.

7.6 calories per serving
.1 gram fat per serving
7 mg sodium per serving
.4 mg cholesterol per serving

◆——SNAPPY——◆
BARBECUE SAUCE

¼ cup onion, finely chopped
2 cloves garlic, minced
1 tablespoon polyunsaturated oil
1 - 8 oz. can tomato sauce
½ cup unsweetened applesauce
2 tablespoons cider vinegar
⅛ teaspoon ground red pepper (cayenne)

In saucepan, sauté onion and garlic in oil until tender. Add remaining ingredients and simmer for 15 minutes. Use sauce over "Barbecued Fish" or "Barbecued Oysters".
Serving suggestions: Leftover sauce freezes well.
Enjoy barbecued fish on french bread using "Snappy Barbecue Sauce" as a topping. Makes 8-2½ tablespoon servings.

30 calories per serving
1.8 grams fat per serving
170 mg sodium per serving
0 mg cholesterol per serving

BARBECUE BASTING SAUCE

2 tablespoons polyunsaturated margarine
½ teaspoon dill weed
¼ teaspoon onion powder
1 tablespoon lemon juice
⅛ teaspoon black pepper

Melt margarine. Add remaining ingredients. Brush on "Barbecued Fish" during the last 2-3 minutes of cooking or pour over "Barbecued Oysters" before serving.
Makes 4 serving.

50 calories per serving
7 grams fat per serving
70 mg sodium per serving
0 mg cholesterol per serving

RATATOUILLE PROVENCALE

4 tomatoes, diced
½ lb. eggplant, diced
1 onion, chopped
1 clove garlic, minced
1 cup white wine or vermouth
1 teaspoon basil
½ teaspoon pepper
oregano (optional)

Sauté tomatoes, eggplant, onions and garlic. Allow the tomatoes to cook down until almost a sauce. Stir in the wine. Add basil, pepper and oregano. Allow to simmer for 10 minutes. Serve with poached fish on a bed of rice. Makes 4 servings.

95 calories per serving
.5 grams fat per serving
5 mg sodium per serving
0 mg cholesterol per serving

◆── ITALIAN SAUCE ──◆

1 tablespoon polyunsaturated oil
1 cup tomato sauce
3 tablespoons white wine
juice of 1 lemon
1 tablespoon wine vinegar
2 cloves garlic, minced
1 teaspoon oregano
1 teaspoon dried mint
2 bay leaves, crushed

Heat oil in skillet or saucepan over moderate heat. Combine remaining ingredients and cook, uncovered, over low heat for 15-20 minutes until slightly thickened. Pour over the steamed fish just before serving or serve in a separate sauceboat. Makes 1¼ cups.

40 calories per serving
2.8 grams fat per serving
260 mg sodium per serving
0 mg cholesterol per serving

◆—— BASIC WHITE ——◆ SAUCE

1 tablespoon polyunsaturated margarine
1 tablespoon flour
white pepper
1 cup skim milk
¼ teaspoon salt (optional)

Melt margarine in a saucepan over low heat. Blend in the flour and pepper to make a roux. Cook on low heat, stirring until the mixture is smooth and bubbly. Stir in the milk and salt. Heat to boiling and cook 1 minute, stirring constantly. Medium-thick white sauce: increase margarine and flour to 2 tablespoons each. For thick sauce, increase to 4 tablespoons each. Makes 4 - ¼ cup servings. Serve over poached or steamed fish.

Basic sauce:
50 calories per serving
3 grams fat per serving
210 mg sodium per serving
0 mg cholesterol per serving

CAPER SAUCE

1 cup plain low fat yogurt
2 tablespoons capers, chopped
1 tablespoon lemon juice
1 tablespoon parsley, chopped
2 teaspoons dried instant minced onion
1 teaspoon lemon rind, grated

Combine all ingredients and mix thoroughly. Chill several hours or overnight. Serve with poached fish. Makes 4 servings.

50 calories per serving
.8 grams fat per serving
90 mg sodium per serving
5 mg cholesterol per serving

◆——LEMON RELISH——◆

¹/₄ cup parsley, chopped
¹/₂ cup green onion, chopped
¹/₄ cup fresh lemon juice

Combine all ingredients in a bowl. Use as an excellent complement to broiled, steamed or sauteed fillets. Makes 1 cup.

3 calories per tablespoon
0 grams fat per tablespoon
0 mg sodium per tablespoon
0 mg cholesterol per tablespoon

THOUSAND ISLAND DRESSING

¼ cup onion, finely chopped
2 cloves garlic, minced
1 tablespoon polyunsaturated oil
1 - 8 oz. can tomato sauce
½ cup unsweetened applesauce
2 tablespoons cider vinegar
⅛ teaspoon ground red pepper (cayenne)
½ cup plain low fat yogurt
¼ cup mayonnaise

In saucepan sauté onion and garlic in oil until tender. Add tomato sauce, unsweetened applesauce, cider vinegar and ground red pepper and simmer for 15 minutes. Cool. Add plain low fat yogurt and mayonnaise. Serve with crab or shrimp louie. Makes 40 tablespoons.

18 calories per tablespoon
1.5 grams fat per tablespoon
43 mg sodium per tablespoon
1 mg cholesterol per tablespoon

◆—LIGHT THOUSAND—◆ ISLAND DRESSING

1 cup low-fat cottage cheese
¼ cup chili sauce
¼ cup plus 2 tablespoons skim milk
1 teaspoon paprika
2 tablespoons celery, finely chopped
2 tablespoons green pepper, finely chopped
2 tablespoons ripe black olives, finely chopped
1 tablespoon sweet pickle relish
1 tablespoon onion, finely chopped
1 tablespoon Parmesan cheese, grated

Combine first 5 ingredients in container of electric blender: process until smooth. Stir in remaining ingredients. Chill. Makes 2 cups.

10 calories per tablespoon
1.8 grams fat per tablespoon
30 mg sodium per tablespoon
1.0 mg cholesterol per tablespoon

SWEDISH CREAM SAUCE

1 cup low fat cottage cheese
¼ cup cucumber, grated
2 tablespoons chives, chopped

Mix ingredients together and chill. Serve with poached or steamed fish. Makes 1¼ cups sauce or 4 servings.

55 calories per serving
1 gram fat per serving
120 mg sodium per serving
5 mg cholesterol per serving

GENERAL INFORMATION

About the Authors

Janis Harsila, R.D. was originator and developer of the "Seafood Is Heart Food" campaign for the American Heart Association which helped to lead to national awareness of seafood and health. Janis is on the leading edge of relating the latest seafood and nutrition research to the consumer and teaches many seminars on the subject. She co-edited a seafood cookbook called, "Seafood Treasures" and is a consulting dietitian for National Seafood Educators.

National Seafood Educator's owner Evie Hansen continues to reign as one of America's leaders in seafood education. Her knowledge and experience in the seafood industry includes working on commercial fishing vessels, in seafood processing plants, a weekly television program on seafood and writing a seafood retail book called "Selling Seafood." The hundreds of seminars and in-store demonstrations represent her speaking, selling and teaching skills. She works with such retailers as Safeway developing promotional programs, training seminars and merchandising strategies.

For more information regarding speeches and seminars, National Seafood Educators may be reached at
P.O. Box 60006 , Richmond Beach, WA 98160
(206) 546-6410

DEFINITIONS

To better understand fat-controlled and low cholesterol diets these definitions may be helpful.

ATHEROSCLEROSIS is a disease in which fatty deposits collect on the inside of the artery wall. These deposits add up over many years, narrowing the channel through which blood flows. Atherosclerosis increases the risk of heart attack and stroke.

CHOLESTEROL is a waxy material used in many of the body's chemical processes. Everyone needs cholesterol for good health, but too much cholesterol in the blood is associated with development of premature coronary heart disease and atherosclerosis. Cholesterol is found only in foods of animal origin, and is also manufactured in the blood. The American Heart Association recommends reducing the daily intake to no more than 300 milligrams of cholesterol from dietary sources.

TRIGLYCERIDES are fats that are carried in the blood and are stored in the body as body fat. Triglycerides are made by your body from foods which you have eaten. Elevated levels of blood triglycerides may damage the blood vessels and increase your chance of developing coronary heart disease.

FAT is the most concentrated source of food energy or calories. Most Americans consume 40 percent or more of their daily calories as fat. The American Heart Association recommends 30 percent or less for better health. Animal sources of protein which are low in fat include SEAFOOD, chicken without skin, turkey and veal. Fats in food are present in three forms: saturated fat, polyunsaturated fat and monosaturated fat.

SATURATED FATS tend to raise the level of cholesterol in the blood and should be restricted in the diet. These are fats that solidify at room temperature. Saturated fats are present in all animal products, particularly beef, lamb, pork, ham and dairy products made from whole milk. Saturated vegetable fats are found in many solid and hydrogenated shortenings and in coconut oil, cocoa butter and palm oil.

POLYUNSATURATED FATS tend to lower the level of cholesterol in the blood. These fats are liquid at room temperature and are usually found in liquid oils of vegetable origin. Oils made from corn, cottonseed, safflower, sesame seed, soybean and sunflower are high in polyunsaturated fats. SEAFOOD oils are high in polyunsaturated fats.

OMEGA-3 FATTYACIDS are long-chained poly-unsaturated fats that tend to lower blood cholesterol and triglyceride levels, as well as, to thin the blood. All fish and shellfish contain omega-3 fatty acids (technically, eicosapentanoic acid (EPA) and docosahexaenoic acid (DHA)).

MONOSATURATED FATS include olive and peanut oil. Latest studies have indicated that monosaturated fats tend to lower blood cholesterol levels.

SODIUM is a mineral present in table salt and most foods. Sodium is often added in the processing of foods. Under certain conditions sodium causes the body to hold water which then causes blood pressure to rise.

BIBLIOGRAPHY

Adams, C.: Nutritive Value of American Foods in Common Units, Agriculture Handbook No. 456, USDA, U.S. Government Printing Office, Washington D.C., 1975.

Kromhout, D., Bosschieter, E. and Coulander, C.: The Inverse Relation Between Fish Consumption and 20-Year Mortality From Coronary Heart Disease. The New England Journal of Medicine, May 9, 1985: 312: 1205-09.

Pennington, J. and Church, H.: Food Values of Portions Commonly Used, Bowes and Church (13th edition). Harper & Row, Publisher, New York, 1980.

Sidwell, V.: Chemical and Nutritional Composition of Finfishes, Whales, Crustaceans, Mollusks, and Their Products, U.S. Dept. of Commerce, NOAA, NMFS, National Technical Information Service, Springfield, VA, 1981.

Stansby, M. and Hall, A.: Chemical Composition of Commercially Important Fish of the United States. Fish and Wildlife Service Fishery Leaflet 116. U.S. Government Printing Office, Washington, D.C., 1967.

Grundy, S., et. al.: Rationale of the Diet-Heart Statement of the American Heart Association, Report of Nutrition Committee, American Heart Association, American Heart Association's Office of Communications, Dallas, Texas, Circulation 65, No. 4, 1982.

United States Department of Fish and Wildlife Service, Bureau of Commercial Fisheries: Guide to Buying Fresh and Frozen Fish and Shellfish.

USDA Provisional Table HNIS/PT-103, 1985.

DESIRABLE WEIGHTS – AGES 25 AND OVER

Weight in Pounds According to Frame (In Indoor Clothing)

———————————————— **Men** ————————————————

Height (with shoes on) 1-inch heels		Small Frame	Medium Frame	Large Frame
Feet	**Inches**			
5	2	112 – 120	118 – 129	126 – 141
5	3	115 – 123	124 – 133	129 – 144
5	4	118 – 126	124 – 136	132 – 148
5	5	121 – 129	127 – 139	135 – 152
5	6	124 – 133	130 – 143	138 – 156
5	7	128 – 137	134 – 147	142 – 161
5	8	132 – 141	138 – 152	147 – 166
5	9	136 – 145	142 – 156	151 – 170
5	10	140 – 150	146 – 160	155 – 174
5	11	144 – 154	150 – 165	159 – 179
6	0	148 – 158	154 – 170	164 – 184
6	1	152 – 162	158 – 175	168 – 189
6	2	156 – 167	162 – 180	173 – 194
6	3	160 – 171	167 – 185	178 – 199
6	4	164 – 175	172 – 190	182 – 204

———————————————— **Women** ————————————————

Height (with shoes on) 1-inch heels		Small Frame	Medium Frame	Large Frame
Feet	**Inches**			
4	10	92 – 98	96 – 107	104 – 119
4	11	94 – 101	98 – 110	106 – 122
5	0	96 – 104	101 – 113	109 – 125
5	1	99 – 107	104 – 116	112 – 128
5	2	102 – 110	107 – 119	115 – 131
5	3	105 – 113	110 – 122	118 – 134
5	4	108 – 116	113 – 126	121 – 138
5	5	111 – 119	116 – 130	125 – 142
5	6	114 – 123	120 – 135	129 – 146
5	7	118 – 127	124 – 139	133 – 150
5	8	122 – 131	128 – 143	137 – 154
5	9	126 – 135	132 – 147	141 – 158
5	10	130 – 140	136 – 151	145 – 163
5	11	134 – 144	140 – 155	149 – 168
6	0	138 – 148	144 – 159	153 – 173

For girls between 18 and 25, subtract 1 pound for each year under 25. Prepared by Metropolitan Life Insurance Co.

ORDER FORM

Please send me ___ copies of SEAFOOD: A Collection of Heart-Healthy Recipes
@ $11.95

or 3 copies . . . . @ $32.95 $ _____

Shipping and Handling ($2.00 per book) $ _____

Wash. residents add .94¢ per book $ _____

Total enclosed $ _____

I enclosed   check ☐ **VISA** money order ☐ MasterCard

Bill my   VISA ☐   Mastercard ☐

Card # _____ Expires _____

Signature _____

Ship to:

Name _____

Address _____

City _____ State _____ Zip _____

Mail this form and payment to:
    Seafood – A Collection of Heart-Healthy Recipes
    National Seafood Educators
    P.O. Box 60006
    Richmond Beach, WA 98160
    (206) 546-6410

Please list bookstores, gift shops or seafood markets in your area that would be interested in handling this cookbook.

INDEX